AF600175

THE PLENARY COUNCIL

THE CATHOLIC UNIVERSITY OF AMERICA
CANON LAW STUDIES
No. 372

The Plenary Council

A HISTORICAL SYNOPSIS AND A COMMENTARY

A DISSERTATION

SUBMITTED TO THE FACULTY OF THE SCHOOL OF CANON LAW
OF THE CATHOLIC UNIVERSITY OF AMERICA IN PARTIAL
FULFILLMENT OF THE REQUIREMENTS FOR THE
DEGREE OF DOCTOR OF CANON LAW

BY THE
REVEREND ELIAS OLARTE POBLETE, J.C.L.
PRIEST OF THE DIOCESE OF LIPA, PHILIPPINES

THE CATHOLIC UNIVERSITY OF AMERICA PRESS
WASHINGTON 17, D. C.
1958

NIHIL OBSTAT:

Eduardus G. Roelker, S.T.D., J.C.D.
Censor Deputatus
Washingtonii, die 3 maii, 1956

IMPRIMATUR:

✠ ALEXANDER A. OLALIA, D.D., J.C.D.
Episcopus Lipensis
Lipae, die 18 maii, 1956

Printed by Theo Gaus' Sons, Inc., Brooklyn 1, N. Y., U. S. A.

To

Our Lady

Of The

Miraculous Medal

FOREWORD

The councils of the Church, admittedly a source of discipline in the Mystical Body of Christ, aid in the government of the faithful by establishing laws, punishing transgressions, and repairing such damages as various occasions and a dissolution of good morals make inevitable. There is no doubt that the work of plenary councils aids greatly in eradicating heresies, in uprooting schisms, in reforming customs and in conserving ecclesiastical traditions. Thus the Church, one and united, but in membership found divided in an expanse of far-away regions, profits from these councils in that unification of action which is fitted to all occasions which it encounters. Under such guidance, the Pastors of the Church can work more fruitfully to safeguard and conserve in their strength and vigor the rules of faith and of discipline. From the constant experience of many centuries it has been discovered that one of the better means of promoting and conserving the mission of the Church is the frequent celebration of plenary councils.

Certainly the most Provident God in His absolute power can conserve His Church in its minutest detail. Nevertheless, God rarely exercises such direct and immediate influence. Instead, He deems it more feasible to allow man, His free and intelligent creature, to aid in the work of salvation by using the very apt means which the same God gives and places in the hands of the Pastors of His Church. In this manner and according to the divine plan the glory of God and the salvation of men are to be happily achieved.

The plenary councils prepare, as it were, the innumerable gains of the Church. They moderate customs and discipline, preserve the unity and integrity of the Church against the attacks of its external and internal foes, and strengthen the Church for the future.

The present treatise is divided into two parts. The first part furnishes a historical synopsis, where the history, origin, and frequency of celebration of plenary councils are exposed in brief. The second part offers a canonical commentary in which 1) the constitution of the plenary council, 2) the sphere of legislation, and 3) the force of the conciliar decrees are analyzed and carefully considered.

In Chapter V, article III, the writer treats of those matters which are of great importance, not only from the standpoint of the subject matter itself, but also and primarily because of their relationship to the present life of the Church in his own beloved country.

The writer wishes to take this occasion to express his profound gratitude to the late Bishop Alfredo F. Verzosa for making it possible to commence the study of Canon Law, to His Excellency, the Most Reverend Alejandro Ayson Olalia, Bishop of Lipa, the Philippines, for his permission to complete that course of study, and to his beloved parents for their kind generosity in making this publication possible. A debt of gratitude is also acknowledged to the members of the Faculty of the School of Canon Law for their gracious and unfailing assistance. To all other friends who have in any way been of assistance in the preparation of this study the writer feels deeply grateful.

TABLE OF CONTENTS

PAGE

FOREWORD ix

PART I

HISTORICAL DEVELOPMENT

CHAPTER I

LEGISLATION BEFORE THE COUNCIL OF TRENT 3
Article 1. History of the Plenary Council 3
Article 2. Origin of the Plenary Council 4
Article 3. Frequency of Celebration 5
A. From the I Council of Nicaea (325) to the Sixth Century 5
B. From the Sixth Century to the Ninth Century.. 6
C. From the IV General Council of the Lateran (1215) to the Council of Trent (1545-1563) ... 7

CHAPTER II

OPERATION OF THE PLENARY COUNCIL 9
Article 1. Convocation and Presidency 9
Article 2. Constituent Members 9
Article 3. Sphere of Legislation 10

CHAPTER III

LEGISLATION FROM THE COUNCIL OF TRENT TO THE CODE... 12
Article 1. Frequency of Celebrating the Plenary Council 12
Article 2. Authority of the Plenary Council............ 14
Article 3. Order and Precedence 15
Article 4. Subject Matter 16
Article 5. Recognition and Promulgation of Decrees.... 17
Article 6. Strength of the Decrees 17
Article 7. Dispensation from the Decrees 18

PART II

Canonical Commentary

CHAPTER IV

The Constitution of the Plenary Council 22
Article 1. Nature of the Plenary Council 23
A. The Concept of the Plenary Council 23
B. The Jurisdictional Authority of the Plenary Council 26
C. Time and Place of Celebration 27
Article 2. Convocation of the Council 29
A. Provision of The Code 29
B. Permission Required for the Celebration 31
C. Presiding Officer 32
Article 3. Members of the Council with Deliberative Vote 33
A. Deliberative Vote Granted by Law 33
1. Local Ordinaries 33
2. Procurators 37
B. Deliberative Vote Accorded by Authority 37
Article 4. Persons in the Plenary Council with Consultative Vote 38
A. Members of the Clergy, Secular and Religious.. 38
B. Procurators 39
Article 5. Obligation of Attendance 40
A. Who must be Present 40
B. Premature Departure 42
Article 6. Precedence 42
A. Its Necessity 42
B. Norms of Precedence at the Plenary Council ... 43
Article 7. Profession of Faith 46
A. The Obligation of the Profession of Faith...... 47
B. Persons Obliged to Make the Profession of Faith 47
C. The Formula to be Used in the Profession of Faith 48

CHAPTER V

Object of Legislation 50
Article 1. Competence of the Council 50
A. Definition of the Code 50
B. Nature of the Competence 51
C. Decisions of the Council 53
Article 2. General Object of Legislation Mentioned in the Code 55
A. Increase of Faith 56
B. Preservation of Morals 57
C. Correction of Abuses 58
D. Settlement of Controversies 58
E. Uniformity of Discipline 59
Article 3. Particular Object of Legislation 60
A. Conferring of Parishes by *Concursus* 61
1. Desire of the Council of Trent 62
2. Means of Expediting the *Concursus* 63
B. Disabled and Aged Priests 64
1. Their Support 64
2. Contributions to Their Support 65
3. Other Means of Support 66
C. Suspended Priests 68
1. House of Penance 69
2. Their Support 70
D. Sacred Music 74
1. Sacred Music in Divine Worship 74
2. Obligation of Pastors 75
E. Catholic Schools 77
1. Establishment of Catholic Schools 78
2. Danger of Non-catholic Schools 80
3. Support of Catholic Schools 82
4. Pastors and Their Duties 85
5. Obligation of Parents 86
6. Influence of Teachers 87

F. Censure and Prohibition of Books 88
1. Censorship 89
2. Prohibition 92

CHAPTER VI

AUTHORITY OF THE CONCILIAR DECREES 94
Article 1. Recognition of the Conciliar Decrees 94
Article 2. Promulgation of the Decrees 97
Article 3. Dispensation from the Conliliar Decrees 101
Article 4. Interpretation of the Conciliar Decrees 104
CONCLUSIONS 107
BIBLIOGRAPHY 109
ABBREVIATIONS 117
APPENDIX 118
ALPHABETICAL INDEX 121
BIOGRAPHICAL NOTE 126
CANON LAW STUDIES 127

PART ONE

Historical Development

CHAPTER I

Legislation Before the Council of Trent

Article 1. History of the Plenary Council

When the bishops of only one patriarchate or primacy (i.e. of a diocese, in the ancient sense of the word), or of only one kingdom or nation, assembled under the presidency of the patriarch, or primate, or first metropolitan, then there was respectively a national, or patriarchal, or primatial council, which frequently received the name of universal or plenary (*universale* or *plenarium*).[1] The plenary council as distinguished from provincial (embracing only one province) and ecumenical (general) councils is the object of this study. A plenary council is the lawful assembly of the ordinaries of several ecclesiastical provinces for the purpose of deliberating upon and decreeing for the ecclesiastical needs.[2]

The word "council" comes from *"conciliare."* Among ecclesiastical authors, the word "council" is found for the first time in Tertullian (ca. 160 - ca. 230).[3] He praised the holding of councils, which he described as a source of edification.[4] Instead of "council," the original Greek term "synod" (συνοδος) appears once in a while

---

[1] Hefele, *A History of the Christian Councils,* tr. by Wm. R. Clark (5 vols., Edinburg: T. & T Clark, 1876-1896), I, pp. 3 & 4, n. 3 (hereafter cited as *A History*).

[2] Wernz, *Ius Decretalium* (6 vols., Vols. I-IV, Romae et Prati, 1908-1915; Vol. I, 3. ed., 1913; Vol. II, 3. ed., 1915; Vol. III, 2. ed., 1908; Vols. V-VI, 1. ed., Ojetti et Vidal, 1913-1914), II, n. 843.

[3] De Jejunio, cap. 13: *"Aguntur praeterea per Graecias illa certis in locis concilia ex universis ecclesiis. . . ."—Corpus Scriptorum Ecclesiasticorum Latinorum* (incomplete, Vindibonae, 1866—), XX, pars I, 292 (hereafter cited as *CSEL*). It may be observed that Tertulian was trained in law and that *concilium* was a term of administrative law.

[4] *Loc. cit.*: *"Et hoc quam dignum fide suspicante congregari undique ad Christum."*

in the early Latin usage of the Church. It is thus found, for example, in the Apostolic Canons.[5]

It was of Apostolic tradition, according to Baronius (1538-1607), that there should be a general assembly of the bishops on the occasion of controversies concerning the Faith, or whenever very difficult matters arose for consideration.[6] So, besides the Ecumenical Councils, from the very beginning of the Christian era, other kinds of councils were celebrated in which bishops of many ecclesiastical provinces convened. This practice began in the third century. These councils were called plenary.

Article 2. Origin of the Plenary Council

The historian Eusebius (263-339) referred vaguely to synods held probably in the early second half of the second century against the Montanists by Apollinaris Claudius of Hierapolis in Phrygia and Sotus of Anchialus in Thrace;[7] he explicitly named several councils for the celebration of which the Easter controversy gave occasion towards the end of the same century in Palestine, Pontus, Mesopotamia, Asia Minor, Gaul and Italy.[8]

In the third century during the periods of peace, bishops met frequently to condemn heresies or settle controversies: in Carthage about the year 220, in Alexandria in 231, in Rome in 235, 251 and

---

[5] Can. 36—Bruns, *Canones Apostolorum et Conciliorum Saeculorum IV-VII* (2 vols., Berolini, 1839), I, 6 (hereafter cited as Bruns).

[6] *Annales Ecclesiastici* (ed. A. Theiner, 37 vols., Vols I-XXVIII, Barri-Ducis, 1864-1875; Vols. XXIX-XXXVII, Parisiis, 1876-1883), II, pp. 351, 352, n. 19 (hereafter cited as *Annales*).

[7] Eusebius, *Historia Ecclesiastica,* Lib. V, n. 19—*Die griechischen christlichen Schriftsteller der ersten drei Jahrhunderte* (7 vols. in 10, Vol. II, pars I (1903), pars II (1906), Leipzig), II, pars I, p. 464, n. 16 (hereafter cited as *GCS*); Ceillier, *Histoire Générale des Auteurs Sacrés et Ecclésiastiques* (14 vols. in 17, Paris, 1858-1896), II, 537 (hereafter cited as *Histoire Générale*); Hefele-Leclercq, *Histoire des Conciles* (nouvelle traduction française, 11 vols. in 21, Paris, 1907-1952), I, 3, 24 (hereafter cited as *Histoire*).

[8] Ceillier, *Histoire Générale,* II, 541; Eusebius, *Historia Ecclesiastica,* Lib. VII, nn. 27, 28—*GCS,* II, pars II, 702, 704.

260, in Iconium from 230-235, and again in Carthage six times between 251 and 256, in Narbonne in 255, and in other places.[9]

The prelates attending these meetings usually belonged to several civil provinces. In the middle of the third century, St. Firmilian, Bishop of Caesarea in Cappadocia (230-268), wrote to St. Cyprian of Carthage (248-258)[10] about synods held every year by the bishops and priests of the provinces of Pontus and Cappadocia. Most probably these were provincial councils; with the progress of provincial organization in the Church they became a regular institution. The Council of Nicaea (325)[11] and of Antioch (341)[12] confirmed and extended an existing discipline when they ordered the metropolitans to call together the bishops of their province twice a year.

For matters of more general interest, bishops continued to assemble from different ecclesiastical provinces even outside of the Ecumenical Councils as, for example, at Elvira about the year 305, at Arles in 314, at Ancyra in 314, and at Hippo in 393. Of special importance were the Plenary Councils of Carthage in the fourth and fifth centuries, and those of Toledo in the sixth and seventh.[13]

Article 3. Frequency of Celebration

A. From the I Council of Nicaea (325) *to the Sixth Century*

The Code[14] includes under the name of Plenary Council all those in which bishops belonging to several provinces take part. Accord-

---

[9] Cf. Mansi, *Sacrorum Conciliorum Nova et Amplissima Collectio* (53 vols. in 60, Paris, Arnhem, Leipzig, 1901-1927), Vol. I (hereafter cited as Mansi).

[10] Litt. 75—Mansi, I, 911.

[11] Can. 5—Mansi, II, 687.

[12] Can. 20—Mansi, II, 1326.

[13] Thomassinus, *Vetus et Nova Ecclesiae Disciplina circa Beneficia et Beneficiarios* (3 partes in 10 vols., ed. postrema cum Parisiensi accuratissime collata, Magontiaci, 1787), Pars II, lib. III, cap. 45, nn. 2, 3 (hereafter cited as *Vetus et Nova Disciplina;* cf. Migne, *Patrologia Cursus Completus, Series Latina* (221 vols.. Parisiis, 1844-1864, IV (hereafter cited as *MPL*).

[14] Canon 281—*Codex Iuris Canonici Pii X Pontificis Maximi iussi digestus Benedicti XV auctoritate promulgatus, Praefatione, Fontium Anno-*

ing to the decree of the Council of Nicaea (325) in its fifth canon, a yearly synod was to be assembled, and two legates or as many as were chosen were to be sent by the primates of every province.[15] The Council held in Hippo in 393 prescribed (can. 5) an annual meeting of the bishops of all the African provinces.[16]

Such importance had the African national or plenary councils attained by the year 397 that the obligation of holding plenary or national councils once a year was decreed by the III Council of Carthage (397) in its second canon.[17] But this obligation proved too onerous, and another Council of Carthage decided that the reunions should take place when circumstances would call for them.[18] This rule prevailed practically everywhere. This was the rise of the national or plenary councils, which flourished first in Africa as early as the fourth century, with their frequency regulated by legislation,[19] as well as the later development of these councils in France and Spain.[20]

B. From the Sixth Century to the Ninth Century

In the year 590, the neglect regarding the celebration of councils was reflected in a letter written by Pope St. Gregory the Great. In this letter the Pope advised the bishops of Sicily to celebrate a council each year for the benefit of the Church, and in consideration of the poor and the oppressed.[21]

---

tatione et Indice Analytico-Alphabetico ab Emo Petro Card. Gasparri Auctus (Romae: Typis Polyglottis Vaticanis, 1917; Reimpressio, 1946).

15 Bruns, I, 15; Hardouin, *Acta Conciliorum et Epistolae Decretales* (12 vols., Parisiis, 1714-1715), I, 326 (hereafter cited as *Acta Conciliorum*).

16 Bruns, I, 136.

17 Bruns, I, 123.

18 *Codex Ecclesiae Africanae*, can. 95: "*Placuit ut non sit ultra fatigandis fratribus anniversaria necessitas, sed quoties exegerit causa communis, id est totius Africae, undecumque ad hanc sedem de hac re datae litterae opportunitas persuaserit; causae autem quae communes non sunt in suis provinciis judicentur.*"—Bruns, I, 184.

19 Hinschius, *Das Kirchenrecht der Katholiken und Protestanten in Deutschland* (6 vols., Berlin, 1869-1897), III, 511 (hereafter cited as *Das Kirchenrecht*).

20 Hinschius, *op. cit.*, III, 7.

21 Lib. I, Ep. 1; Lib. III, Ep. 57; Lib. IX, Ep. 222—*Monumenta Ger-*

The same Pope wrote also to the Frankish kings with the request that they use their influence to encourage the holding of councils.[22] The monarchs who appreciated the influence of the councils, particularly the Carolingian princes, urged, if they did not also command, their frequent and even, for a while, annual and bi-annual celebration.[23]

It was said that national councils,[24] to which Charlemagne († 814) gave his support and influence, were held with great frequency.[25]

C. *From the IV General Council of the Lateran* (1215) *to the Council of Trent* (1545-1563)

Pope Innocent III (1192-1216), seeing the loose discipline in the Church, attempted a wholesome reform within it. In the IV General Council of the Lateran (1215), which he himself convoked, the same Pope adopted resolutions regarding ecclesiastical discipline, episcopal elections, the election of clerics and the celebrations of councils. Hostiensis († 1271) in his commentary on the celebration of the councils stated that these were to be celebrated every other year.[26] In the next century, Pope Urban V (1362-1370) requested from all archbishops a report on the proceedings of the councils, the celebration of which he urged.[27]

Concerning the celebration of councils every three years, a new statute was issued during the fifteenth century by Pope Martin V. The Pope himself approved it.[28] The V General Council of the

maniae Historica, Gregorii I Papae Registrum Epistolarum (2 vols. in 4, Berolini: Apud Weidmanos, Vol. I, pars I (1891), Vol. II, pars I (1893), Vol. II, pars II (1899), Vol. I, pars I, pp. 1-2 and pp. 216-217; Vol. II, pars I, pp. 213-214 (hereafter cited as *MGH, Registrum*).

[22] Lib. XI, Epp. 50 & 51—*MGM, Registrum*, Vol. II, pars II, pp. 322-324.

[23] Thomassinus, *Vetus et Nova Disciplina*, Pars II, Lib. III, cap. 51.

[24] Hefele-Leclercq, *Histoire*, III, 1123, 1117, 1129, 1133.

[25] Thomassinus, *op. cit.*, Pars II, Lib. III, cap. 52, n. 5.

[26] Hostiensis (Henricus de Segusio † 1271), *Commentaria in Quinque Decretalium Libros* (5 vols. in 3, Venetiis, 1581), Lib. V, tit. I, *de accusationibus, et denuntiationibus*, cap. 25, n. 1 (hereafter cited as *Commentaria*).

[27] Baronius, *Annales*, XXVII, p. 100, 23.

[28] Wernz, *Ius Decretalium*, II, n. 853.

Lateran (1511-1517) had this kind of ruling also.[29] Finally it was inserted in the Constitution *"Regimini Universalis"* by Pope Leo X (1513-1521) on May 4, 1515.[30]

It was indeed from the very beginning of the Church that the celebration of the plenary councils became a constant practice and the enforcement of its laws an efficient means of administration.

---

[29] Sess. X......Mansi, XXXII, 901-939.

[30] N. 12—*Codicis Iuris Canonici Fontes,* cura Emi Petri Card. Gasparri editi (9 vols., Romae: Typis Polyglottis Vaticanis, 1923-1939. Vols. VII-IX, ed. cura et studio Emi Iustiniani Card. Serédi), n. 66 (hereafter cited as *Fontes*).

CHAPTER II

Operation of the Plenary Council

(Before the Council of Trent)

Most of the features connected with the operation of the plenary council remained essentially unchanged through the centuries. This accounts for the relative scarcity of relevant legislation, in the *Corpus Iuris Canonici,* regarding the plenary council, which reached its complete formation at an early stage in the history of the Church.

Article 1. Convocation and Presidency

The convocation of and presidency over plenary councils in the ancient Church belonged by right to Patriarchs, Exarchs or Primates; thus ordinarily, though not always, the Bishops of Carthage convoked the Councils of Africa, the Primate of Toledo those of Spain, the Primate of Arles those of Southern Gaul. Christian Kings, particularly in Spain and France, often also claimed some right of convoking national and, occasionally but not so frequently, provincial councils.[1]

Article 2. Constituent Members

The Council of Nicaea (325), like the subsequent ones, imposed only on bishops the obligation of attending the provincial assemblies;[2] others, however, referred also to the presence of priests, of deacons, and even of laymen. According to Eusebius (263-339),

---

[1] Magnin, *L'Eglise Wisigothique au VIIe Siècle,* I (Paris: A. Picard et Fils, 1912), pp. 51 & 106.

[2] Council of Nicaea (325), can. 5—Bruns, I, 15; c. 3, D. XVIII; IV Council of Toledo (633), can. 4—Bruns, I, 222; *Glossa ordinaria,* c. 1, C. XV, q. 7, ad v. *Concilii;* Ceillier, *Histoire Générale,* II, 432; Fagnanus, *Commentaria in Quinque Decretalium Libros* (5 vols. in 4, Venetiis, 1709), Lib. V, tit. 1, cap. 25, n. 34, p. 26 (hereafter cited as *Commentaria*).

between seventy and eighty bishops assisted at the Council of Antioch in 269, besides priests and deacons.[3]

The Synod of Elvira, celebrated approximately in the year 305, opened in the presence of nineteen bishops, of twenty-six priests, of deacons also and lay people;[4] thirty-three bishops, fifteen priests, twenty-eight deacons, two lectors, and seven exorcists subscribed the Acts of the Council of Arles in the year 314.[5] The IV National Council of Toledo (633) described in detail the order of precedence therein observed; first came the bishops, then the priests, thereupon the deacons, who remained standing, and finally such lay people as had merited admission.[6] Some laymen appeared before councils for personal matters. There may also have been sessions open to the general public. In all cases, however, the bishops alone had a decisive vote, with possibly some priests admitted by the Metropolitan to take part in the deliberations.

Article 3. Sphere of Legislation

In the early Church there were frequent and pressing demands for conciliar activity.[7] Matters treated by the ancient councils, according to the discipline then prevailing, embraced a wide field, extending in particular to questions concerning the election of bishops.[8] With the progress of the years and the formation of a body of laws the field of new conciliar legislation naturally became

---

[3] Eusebius, *Historia Ecclesiastica,* Lib. VII, n. 30—GCS, II, pars II, 730-731.

[4] Hardouin, *Acta Conciliorum,* I, 250.

[5] Hardouin, *op. cit.,* I, 266-267.

[6] IV Council of Toledo (633), can. 4—Bruns, I, 222.

[7] E. g., from the Council of Elvira (305) the following canons were later received into the *Corpus Iuris Canonici*: Can. 52 (apud Bruns, I, 8), as c. 3, C. V. q. 1; can. 54 (apud Bruns, I, 9), as c. 1, C. XXXI, c. 3; can. 72 (apud Bruns, I, 11) as c. 7, C. XXXI, q. 1; can. 73 (apud Bruns, I, 11), as c. 6, C. V, q. 6.

[8] I Council of Nicaea (325), can. 4—Bruns, I, 15; Council of Antioch (341), can. 19—Bruns, I, 85; Mansi, II, 1316; Wernz-Vidal, *Ius Canonicum* (7 vols. in 8, Romae: Apud Aedes Universitatis Gregorianae, 1934-1952; Vol. II, 3. ed., 1943; Vol. IV, Pars II, 1, ed., 1935; Vol. VII, 2. ed., 1951), II, 671, 672.

limited. In every century, however, national problems which arose in a particular area had to be met with national or plenary legislation. In a nation this was the office of the plenary councils. Obviously the plenary councils had only national jurisdiction, but their laws were binding upon the whole nation or territory.[9]

What developed into the chief sphere of plenary legislation was the office of correction. Upon the plenary council, through the centuries, devolved the responsibility of correcting aberrations from the law by means of specific provisions adapted to the time and place. As the necessity of making new laws grew with the formation of a stable body of laws, the function of corrective legislation became more and more important.

The Church, desirous of safeguarding the reputation of its clergy, through the IV Council of Carthage, held in 398, enjoined continence upon all priests and deacons[10] Thus, what was at first a generally observed counsel became a strict duty, at least in the West.

The Council of Mileve (402) attacked and condemned the Pelagian errors.[11] The Council of Orange (529) discussed and condemned Semi-Pelagianism.[12]

Finally, it was not enough to have a practical body of laws. That law had to be well known and had to be universally applied to become effective. The publication of the law and the practical insistence upon it in a given territory made the jurisdictional responsibility of the plenary council a function which became of great importance.

---

[9] I Ecumenical Council of Constantinople (381), can. 2—Mansi, III, 560.

[10] Hardouin, *Acta Conciliorum*, I, 982.

[11] Caranza, *Summa Conciliorum* (Duaci, 1639), pp. 211-221.

[12] Hardouin, *op. cit.*, I, 1097-1102.

CHAPTER III

Legislation from the Council of Trent to the Code

Article 1. Frequency of Celebrating the Plenary Council

The Church is extremely cautious, and the motives of its policy are historical. From its infancy the Church has been engaged in defending its rightful supremacy in spiritual matters. One of the most pernicious forms of attack the temporal rulers have used to resist the papal power has been the attempt to secure a measure of control over local or particular councils.

In the sixteenth century, among the abuses reigning in France, was the so-called right of the Christian Kings to call for a National Council. With such right the Kings of France practically gathered in a Council the whole clergy of France.[1] The problem became more acute especially after the Reformation, when the temporal rulers looked to such gatherings for support against the popes themselves. This practice, however illegitimate, or perhaps justified only by exceptional circumstances, gave an apparent foundation to the theory of the King's power over National Councils so stronly advocated by the Gallicans, by Febronius († 1790) and his followers, and Nuytz († 1856) and the Regalists. The popes condemned their teachings repeatedly, denying to civil governments any rights in this matter[2] Hence, the exaggerated Nationalism condemned by Pope Pius XI is not of this century alone.[3]

In the seventeenth and eighteenth centuries, in France, there was a glaring example of resistance to papal authority in the *Comitia Cleri Gallicani.* The Assembly of 1681 refused to accept

---

[1] Bouix, *De Concilio Provinciali* (3. ed., Parisiis, 1884), pp. 49 ff. (hereafter cited as *Concilio Provinciali*).

[2] Pius VI, const. *Auctorem Fidei,* 28 aug. 1794, prop. Synodi Pistorien. damn.—*Fontes,* n. 475.; Denzinger-Bannwart-Umberg, *Enchiridion Symbolorum, Definitionum et Declarationum de Rebus Fidei et Morum* (26. ed., Friburgi Brisgoviae: Herder & Co., 1947), nn. 1735; 1736; 1737.

[3] *Acta Apostolicae Sedis, Commentarium Officiale* (Romae, 1909—), XVI (1924), 8-10 (hereafter cited as *AAS*).

the intervention of Pope Innocent XI (1676-1689), who had condemned the extension of the *regalia,* and questioned an uncanonical appointment of the royalist Archbishop de Harlay († 1695).[4] The second assembly of 1682 formulated the noted Four Gallican Articles, which rendered nugatory the exercise of supreme papal jurisdiction within the French Church.[5] The Synod of Pistoia (1786) convoked by the regalist Bishop de Ricci († 1810), adopted the Four Gallican Articles of 1682, and claimed many rights for the civil power.[6] The Pistoian decrees received royal sanction, and Leopold II, Grand Duke of Tuscany († 1792), convened a Synod of the Tuscan Bishops to have them approved.[7]

The attacks against the Church were resumed in France when Pope Pius VII (1800-1823) was made a prisoner. During the time of his imprisonment the Pope refused to institute French bishops; he did so only after he was liberated. In 1809, the Council convoked by Napoleon was led under pressure to declare that canonical institution of a bishop given by a Metropolitan might possibly be recognized by a National Council, as provisionally a substitute for the pontifical bulls.[8] Another council at Paris, two years later, dominated by the instructions of Napoleon, decreed that the canonical institution was to be given within six months by the Pope, or, if the Pope failed to do so, by the Metropolitan. Nevertheless, the intrepid Pontiff refused to recognize it as a National Council.[9]

In the nineteenth century this appropriated power of the kings to call plenary or national councils was after many years effectively suppressed, when a negative answer was given by Pope Pius IX in February, 1849, to the request of the Bishops of France

---

4 *Acta et Decreta Sacrorum Conciliorum Recentiorum, Collectio Lacensis* (7 vols., auctoribus G. Schneemann Vols. I-VI et T. Granderath Vol. VII, Friburgi Brisgoviae, 1870-1892), I, 808-810 (hereafter cited as *Coll. Lac.*); Mansi, XXXVI, 831.

5 *Coll. Lac.,* I, 831.

6 Mansi, XXXVIII, 989-1282.

7 *Loc. cit.*

8 Mansi, XXXIX, 85-87.

9 *Coll. Lac.* IV, 1228-1232; Mansi, XXXIX, 88-92.

to celebrate a Plenary Council for the whole of France.[10] Pope Pius IX explicitly declared that his permission was necessary to hold such a council.[11] The Bishops of Germany received the same kind of answer in May 17, 1849, when they asked for the permission to celebrate a plenary council,[12] but later on the former practice of celebrating plenary councils was followed again. Many plenary councils have been celebrated since then. Among these were the Plenary Councils of Baltimore in 1852, 1866[13] and 1884; the Plenary Synod of Ireland in the year 1875; the Plenary Councils of Australia in 1885, 1895 and 1905, and also the Plenary Council of Latin America in 1899.[14] Certainly the Bishops of France during the Council of the Vatican asked that a Plenary Council of the bishops and their people might be called so that the laws for the celebrating or conducting of a plenary council could become clearly established.[15]

Article 2. Authority of the Plenary Council

Plenary Councils had true legislative power, which was superior to that of any individual bishop or metropolitan who was a member of the council.[16] From the exercise of this power many and singular benefits derived. The legislation of a plenary council could serve as a check upon evil and a power for good.[17]

Though plenary councils could be of relatively intermediate importance, yet among local councils they held the highest place.[18] Their authority was original, not delegated. It combined effec-

---

[10] *Coll. Lac.*, IV, 2.

[11] *Coll. Lac.*, IV, 4; V, 995 & 1336.

[12] *Coll. Lac., V*, 994-996.

[13] *Coll. Lac.*, III, 129; 1143; 323; 1247.

[14] Wernz-Vidal, *Ius Canonicum*, II, p. 675, nota 33.

[15] Martin, *Omnium Concilii Vaticani Quae ad Doctrinam et Disciplinam pertinet Documentorum Collectio* (Paderbornae, 1873), pp. 157 ff.

[16] S. C. S. Off., 10 sept. 1896, ad 1, 2—*Fontes*, n. 1184; cf. also canon 291, § 2.

[17] Pius IX, ep. encycl. *Cum nuper*, 20 ian. 1858, n. 4—*Fontes*, n. 523.

[18] Guilday, *The National Pastorals of the American Hierarchy* (Westminster, Maryland: The Newman Press, 1954), p. 199 (hereafter cited as *National Pastorals*).

tively the benefits of local legislation and of central authority in an eminently practical way.[19] And that unity which is the chief mark of the divinely founded Church became most strikingly apparent to those outside the fold when there was uniformity even, so far as possible, in matters of discipline, and this was a specific end of legislation.[20]

Thus it is that through the long centuries of its legislative history, even to the present day, the Church has in the celebration of plenary councils reflected its solicitude for the observance of the sacred canons and has therein merited high praise from its Supreme Pontiffs.[21]

Article 3. Order and Precedence

A rule which must be followed by each member regarding the proper order of precedence must exist in every well-disciplined society so that the honor which is due to everyone be given, and so that contentions may be avoided. This right, which is derived from the constituted order in the Church, exists as an element that is compatible with any moral or physical person. Precedence is established according to the general principles, which nevertheless look to and even are modified by many special norms. Thus the precedence of the pope has its peculiar norms, particular rules and specific traditions. Thus, therefore, precedence among the members in attendance at a council is indicated as something quite proper, if not also necessary.[22]

The Sovereign Pontiff appoints a representative of his own authority in the Apostolic Legate whom he commissions to preside over the plenary councils.[23]

---

[19] Pastoral Letter, II Plenary Council of Baltimore (1866)—*Coll. Lac.*, III, 1249, b.

[20] S. C. de Prop. Fide, litt. encycl. (ad Epp. Indiar.) 28 aug. 1893—*Collectanea S. Congregationis de Propaganda Fide* (2 vols., Romae: Typographia Polyglotta de Propaganda Fide, 1907), II, n. 1484 (hereafter cited as *Collectanea*).

[21] *Fontes*, n. 4928.

[22] Pius X, const. *Sapienti consilio*, 29 iun. 1908, I, n. 8—*Fontes*, n. 682.

[23] *Coll. Lac.*, III, 1428-1429; The Pastoral Letter of 1884 by the American Hierarchy: "Such, too, has been the expressed wish and injunction of

Article 4. Subject Matter

The laws which a plenary council could enact are certainly not those which belong to dogmatic controversies.[24] The plenary councils must solemnly receive and announce the dogmatic definitions of the Ecumenical Councils and the Roman Pontiffs, and these dogmas must be recommended with great solicitude,[25] but plenary councils must not affirm and publish these dogmas as its own. Catholic doctrines, though formerly they had to some degree been doubtful, could later of course be proposed.[26]

Plenary councils were ordinarily not to define the doctrine of the Church, although they furnished suitable occasions to the assembled bishops for making authoritative statements regarding these teachings. The principal object was that of regulating discipline, whether through the correction of abuses, or through the establishment of such rules of conduct as circumstances required.[27]

The advancement of the interests of the Church of God likewise served as an object for plenary councils. Thus, shortly after the close of the deadly conflict in America between the North and the South, the II Plenary Council in the United States was called by Archbishop Martin Spalding of Baltimore on March 19, 1866.[28]

---

our Holy Father Leo XIII, happily reigning, to whom, as Supreme Pontiff and successor of the Prince of the Apostles, by inherent right belongs the power of convoking this our Third National or Plenary Council, and of appointing (as he has graciously done) an Apostolic Delegate to preside over its deliberations."—Guilday, *National Pastorals*, p. 228.

[24] Benedictus XIV, *De Synodo Dioecesana* (novissima editio, 4 vols., Mechliniae, 1842), Tomus III, Lib. XIII, cap. 3, nn. 1-2, pp. 13-14 (hereafter cited as *De Synodo*).

[25] Sess. XXV, de ref., c. 2—*Concilium Tridentinum, Diariorum, Actorum, Epistolarum, Tractatuum, Nova Collectio* (Edidit Societas Goerresiana, 13 vols., Friburgi Brisgoviae: B. Herder, 1901-1950).

[26] *Coll. Lac.*, VI, *in praefatione*, 3-7.

[27] *Coll. Lac.*, III, 1428-1429.

[28] Cf. Guilday, *National Pastorals*, p. 197: "That at the close of the national crisis, which had acted as a dissolvent upon all sectarian ecclesiastical institutions, the Catholic Church might present to the country and the world a striking proof of the strong bond of unity with which her members are knit together."

Article 5. Recognition and Promulgation of Decrees

Inasmuch as many of the councils of the Church sought to effect a condemnation of the growing heresies of the times, it was necessary that the acts of each council be sent to the Holy See, so that with the authority of the latter the acts of the council might be received by all. This was done not so much for the purpose of attaching to them a still higher authority, but rather for the purpose of guarding against any inaccuracy in the doctrinal discipline of the Church, or any enactment which might be contrary to the spirit of ecclesiastical legislation.[29]

Since the time of Sixtus V (1587) this has been the law. Since that time, at the close of every plenary council, the presiding prelate must forward the Acts and Decrees to the Holy See for revision and recognition before promulgation.[30] The Congregation of the Council, to which Sixtus V entrusted this work, was carefully to study the Acts to see if they contained anything contrary to or simply something in addition to the common law. This, however, did not imply confirmation of all the decisions of the Council, for such decisions did not become papal laws, nor did they receive binding force if they happened to be in themselves invalid.[31] The recognition had, however, some effect; it guaranteed the canonical character of the council, and the substantial value of its provisions.[32]

The promulgation of the laws enacted in the plenary councils belonged to the Apostolic Legate who presided over the council. Once these laws were promulgated, they began to oblige.[33]

Article 6. Strength of the Decrees

The decrees of the plenary councils enjoyed, from the time of their promulgation, the character of ecclesiastical law for the faith-

---

29 *Coll. Lac.*, III, 1249, b.

30 *Coll. Lac.*, II, 66; 1410.

31 Benedictus XIV, *De Synodo*, Lib. III, cap. 3, nn. 1 ff.

32 Nilles, *Commentaria in Concilium Plenarium Baltimorense Tertium ex Praelectionibus Academicis Excerpta* (Oeniponte: C. Pustet, 1888), Pars I, pp. 36 ff. (hereafter cited as *Commentaria*).

33 *Fontes*, n. 1184.

ful in the district or region subject to the jurisdiction of the bishops by whom they had been enacted.[34] Therefore all those who in any way disobeyed or broke the laws established in these councils were to be punished according to the statutes prescribed by the same councils or by the sacred canons. These lawbreakers had to be admonished to obey thenceforth the decrees of such councils, under threat of reprisal with the appropriate remedies of the law, even with censures and other penalties.[35]

The Church, ever solicitous about the salvation of all of its members, has permitted the celebration of plenary councils, because the decrees of these councils are means by which men can learn with entire certainty the truths God require them to believe and the duties He imposes in order that they be saved.[36]

This, however, is not alone the strength and major force of the decrees of a plenary council. Any law or custom, whether provincial, diocesan, or local, even though immemorial, if it was contrary to the decrees of a plenary council, was abrogated, with the exception of any and every particular ruling deriving by indult from the Holy See. Nevertheless a recourse to the Holy See was permitted in a matter of this kind.[37]

Article 7. Dispensation from the Decrees

Although every council commanded the full observance of its legislation, nevertheless, in some extraordinary cases, dispensations were given regarding the fulfillment of a particular law. Dispensations were not to be easily conceded, except for grave reasons which arose from the necessity of the faithful.[38]

The Plenary Council of the Latin American countries was even benign regarding dispensations from its decrees. If there arose a prudent doubt regarding the execution and interpretation of a

---

[34] *Coll. Lac.*, III, 1249, b.

[35] *Coll. Lac.*, VI, 212, b.

[36] Guilday, *National Pastorals*, p. 203.

[37] *Acta et Decreta Concilii Plenarii Americae Latinae* (1899) (Romae: Typis Vaticanis, 1902), Titulum XVI, Caput unicum, n. 995.

[38] *Coll. Lac.*, II, 583.

decree or of several decrees, then, as long as the essence and strength of the said decrees was not affected, the solution of the difficulty was to be sought from the Metropolitans, or from the respective Bishops, if the difficulties were of minor importance. In other cases it was necessary to interpose the recourse to the Sacred Congregation of Extraordinary Ecclesiastical Affairs.[39]

---

39 *Acta et Decreta Concilii Plenarii Americae Latinae, loc cit.*

PART TWO

Canonical Commentary

CHAPTER IV

The Constitution of the Plenary Council

Article 1. Nature of the Plenary Council

A. The Concept of the Plenary Council

When, in 1917, the Code of Canon Law[1] appeared, the attention of many jurists was especially drawn to the ecclesiastical legislation regarding local or particular customs.[2] Then, again, the concern shown by the new Code for local conditions is made manifest in its regulation on the qualities requisite for the episcopal candidacy.[3] The law's provision for local legislation gives consideration to the needs of time, place, and people. Ultimately a law affects and, in turn, is affected by local circumstances. Thus, the need for local legislation.

The Church knows well that the mere accumulation of precepts and prohibitions makes for confusion of discipline. The Church knows also that the sanctification of its children is often hindered by the obstacles which arise from a wide discrepancy of discipline. Thus the Church has ever regarded the plenary council as an effective means for the attainment of the desired uniformity of discipline, the while the particularities of local conditions are duly safeguarded. The Roman Pontiffs have consistently encouraged the celebration of such councils. The Church admirably has expressed its mind in an encyclical letter to a group of bishops who were about to assemble as a legislative body.[4]

---

[1] *Codex Iuris Canonici, Pii X Pontificis Maximi iussu digestus, Benedicti XV auctoritate promulgatus, Praefatione, Fontium Annotatione et Indice Analytico-Alphabetico ab Emo Petro Card. Gasparri Auctus* (Romae: Typis Polyglottis Vaticanis, 1917; Reimpressio, 1946).

[2] Canon 5.

[3] Canon 331, § 1, n. 4: Bonis moribus, pietate, animarum zelo, prudentia, ceterisque dotibus praeditus, *quae ipsum aptum efficiant ad gubernandam dioecesim de qua agatur.*

[4] S. C. de Prop. Fide, litt. encycl. (ad Ep. Indiar.), 28 aug. 1893: "revocare sufficiat . . . ut quantum fieri poterit, in regulis ac normis ad discipli-

A council, in general parlance, is a meeting of clerics held under the authority of a prelate for the transaction of business pertaining to the welfare of the Church. Specifically it is an assembly of bishops and other prelates of the Church for the purpose of discussing and providing legislation on ecclesiastical matters.[5] If this assembly is composed of the bishops and the major prelates of the whole Church who are in union with the Holy See, and is convoked by the Roman Pontiff for the purpose of discussing and deliberating on matters concerning the Universal Church under the headship of the Roman Pontiff,[6] it is called an ecumenical council. Aside from the ecumenical or general council, there are also the particular councils, in which only a part of the Church is represented.[7] The Code, however, does not use the term "general" in its classification. It just states the names ecumenical,[8] plenary[9] and provincial.[10]

A plenary council denotes a meeting of the ordinaries of several ecclesiastical provinces under the presidency of a delegate of the Holy See,[11] while the provincial council is a meeting of the bishops of an ecclesiastical province under the presidency of the metropolitan or senior bishop.[12] Plenary councils possess a higher and a

---

nam spectantibus maxima inducatur et servetur uniformitas, ut exinde quoque praecipua Ecclesiae Christi nota, ex unitate dimanans, luculentius ubique appareat, ac simul admiratio praecaveatur quae ex disciplinas discrepantia facile inter fideles exoritur."—*Fontes,* n. 4928.

[5] Beste, *Introductio in Codicem* (3 ed., Collegeville, Minnesota: St. John's Abbey Press, 1946, p. 234 (hereafter cited as *Introductio*).

[6] Abbo-Hannan, *The Sacred Canons* (2 vols., St. Louis: Herder, 1925), I, 288.

[7] Vermeersch-Creusen, *Epitome Iuris Canonici* (3 vols., Vol. I, 7. ed., Romae: H. Dessain, 1949), I, n. 394 (hereafter cited as *Epitome*).

[8] Canon 222.

[9] Canon 281.

[10] Canon 283.

[11] Coronata, *Institutiones Iuris Canonici Ad Usum Utriusque Cleri et Scholarum* (5 vols., Taurini-Marietti, 1948-1952; Vols. I & II, 4. ed., 1950; Vol. III, 3. ed., 1948; Vol. IV, 3. ed., 1948; Vol. V, 3. ed., 1952), I, n. 368 (hereafter cited as *Institutiones*).

[12] Abbo-Hannan, *op cit.*, I, 328.

more extensive jurisdiction than do provincial councils.[13] As indicated in canon 281, a plenary council requires for its celebration the permission of the Holy Father and it also presupposes that the Holy Father's own legate convokes the council and presides over it. It is thus distinguished from the provincial council, not only in the more intimate participation in its proceedings on the part of the Holy See and in its authority, but also in the fact that its laws bind more than one ecclesiastical province. It is worthy of note that it is not required that all the ecclesiastical provinces of a nation participate in a council before such a council can rightfully be designated as a plenary council. The territory which is governed by plenary legislation is usually, but not necessarily, coterminous with a nation. But when a plenary council is attended by the ordinaries of all the ecclesiastical provinces of a nation it is called a national council.[14] Thus, any council which embraces more than one ecclesiastical province and is at the same time less than an ecumenical (general) council of the Church is a plenary council.[15]

The term "national council," so frequently used in informal conversation, and appearing in Catholic newspapers, is not found in the Code, nor does it occur in the papal documents of today. The eminent jurist Chelodi (1880-1922), having noted that the loyalty of the bishops can be depended on in our time, keenly observed: "Sancta Sedes iterum permisit concilia plenaria, quae sane etiam nationalia esse possunt, at ius ab hoc nomine abstinet."[16] In the United States of America the first national or plenary council was convoked by the Archbishop of Baltimore, Francis P. Kenrick, in his capacity of apostolic delegate of Pope Pius IX (1846-1878).[17]

The plenary council represents the most solemn form of particular ecclesiastical legislation. In it the ordinaries of the several

---

[13] Toso, *Ad Codicem Juris Canonici Commentaria Minora* (5 vols., Romae, 1921-1927), III, 103 (hereafter cited as *Commentaria Minora*).

[14] Vermeersch-Creusen, *Epitome*, I, n. 394.

[15] Toso, *Commentaria Minora*, III, 103.

[16] *Ius de Personis iuxta Codicem Iuris Canonici* (3. ed. curavit Pius Ciprotti, Vicenza: Società Anonima Tipografica, 1942), 374 (hereafter cited as *Ius de Personis*).

[17] Abbo-Hannan, *The Sacred Canons*, I, 328.

ecclesiastical provinces are the joint legislators. Its celebration is truly an epoch-making event in the ecclesiastical history of the nation in which it is held.

B. The Jurisdictional Authority of the Plenary Council

A moral person implies a juridical entity, a subject of rights, distinct from all physical or natural persons. Such a person comes into being either by divine institution or by ecclesiastical law, i.e., by the very enactment of the law itself or by a special concession of the competent ecclesiastical superior through a formal decree, for religious or charitable purposes.[18] A moral person is called collegiate if it is made up of a "college" or group of natural physical persons;[19] thus a collegiate moral person is a juridical entity to which by a formal concession the law attributes a juristic personality, perpetual by nature, existing independently of the physical persons who unite to form it, and possessing the rights and obligations of a moral person or juridical entity.[20]

Concerning collegiate moral persons, the Code has canonized the legal phrase, *tres faciunt collegium,*[21] i.e., every collegiate moral person must at the moment of its formation consist of at least three physical persons. The word *collegium,* in the cited axiom, meant corporation in the early Roman Law;[22] today, however, in the

[18] Cf. canon 100, § 1.

[19] Bouscaren-Ellis, *Canon Law, A Text and Commentary* (2. ed., Milwaukee: Bruce, 1951), p. 86 (hereafter cited as *Canon Law*).

[20] Maroto, *Institutiones Iuris Canonici ad Norman Codicis* (2 vols., Matriti-Romae-Barcinone, 1918-1919), I, 536 (hereafter cited as *Institutiones*): "... persona moralis ... definiri potest: ens juridicum, independenter a personis singularibus ex concessione iuris subsistens atque capacitate iuris acquirendi excercendique donatum."

[21] "... ad congregationem, seu collegium initio constituendum tres ut minimum personas requiri; si tamen illud semel sit constitutum, conservari posse collegium, ejusque jura etiam in duobus, immo in uno."—Schmalzgrueber, *Jus Ecclesiasticum Universum* (5 vols. in 12, Romae, 1843-1845), lib. I, tit. 6, n. 8 (hereafter cited as *Jus Ecclesiasticum*); Canon 100, § 2: Persona moralis collegialis constitui non potest, nisi ex tribus saltem personis physicis.

[22] Brown, *The Canonical Juristic Personality with Special Reference to Its Status in the United States of America,* The Catholic University of America Canon Law Studies, n. 39 (Washington, D. C.: The Catholic Uni-

common usage of canonists,[23] it is understood in the sense of a collegiate moral person. Is the plenary council a collegiate moral person?

Perpetuity by nature[24] is the prerequisite element which eliminates the plenary council as a collegiate moral person. Proofs are not needed to illustrate this statement. It is obvious that the plenary council is transitory, then, not perpetual at all. Hence, a plenary council is not a collegiate moral person, but can it be concluded, therefore, that it does not have any juristic personality?

A plenary council is indeed similar to a *collegium* because of the jurisdictional authority bestowed on the members as a group. Moreover, even in this case the council's jurisdictional power is distinct from that of the physical persons who compose it. In a similar manner, also, the majority vote which produces the acts of the collegiate person[25] has always been the determining norm of conciliar decisions.[26] Plenary councils, therefore, in their similarity to any collegiate moral person are entitled to act with jurisdictional authority.

C. Time and Place of Celebration

The question arises whether the time and place for the celebration of a plenary council is or is not determined by law. When the nature of the plenary council is considered it appears that the designation of time and place is not a matter to be specifically determined by the law. Canon 281 simply states that a plenary council cannot be celebrated without the permission of the Roman Pontiff,[27] i.e., the Holy Father himself must approve the time and the

---

versity of America, 1927), p. 65 (hereafter cited as *Canonical Juristic Personality*).

[23] Cf. Michiels, *Principia Generalia de Personis in Ecclesia* (Lublin: Universitas Catholica, 1932), pp. 318, 333 (hereafter cited as *De Personis*); Maroto, *Institutiones,* I, 546; Wernz-Vidal, *Ius Canonicum,* II, 34-35; Beste, *Introductio,* p. 162.

[24] Canon 102, § 1.

[25] Cf. canon 101, §1, n. 1.

[26] Coronata, *Institutiones,* p. 423; Chelodi, *Ius de Personis,* p. 374.

[27] "Ordinarii plurium provinciarum ecclesiasticarum in Concilium plenarium convenire possunt, petita tamen venia a Romano Pontifice...."

place selected, or designate another time and place in lieu of the former. It follows, therefore, that only in an indirect way the law determines when and where the plenary council is to be held.

There have been exceptions to this general norm, however. In Italy, where many archbishops were without suffragan sees, and hence could not strictly or properly hold provincial councils, they were allowed instead to celebrate a regional plenary council every twenty years.[28] In another instance, the Sacred Congregation of the Consistory, on March 22, 1919, notified the Bishops of Italy that with the exception of the regions or ecclesiastical provinces of Venice, Milan, Turin, Genoa and Rome, plenary and regional councils were to be celebrated instead of provincial councils because of the difficulties involved regarding a certified determination of the boundaries of Italian dioceses.[29]

The Code itself contains no special provision regarding the place of meeting for plenary councils. It leaves such a determination to the decision of the Pontifical Delegate.[30] The Apostolic Legate, nevertheless, must be guided by the demands of reason and justice in selecting the time for the celebration of a plenary council. He should not ordinarily set the time of the council when the law demands the presence of the metropolitan's and bishops in their own territories, for example, during the time of Advent and Lent, and on the feasts of Easter, Pentecost and Corpus Christi.[31] Although it is difficult to foresee circumstances under which the celebration of the council could not be postponed for a short time, v. g., during Lent, yet the aforesaid canon allows exceptions of a grave and urgent type to the stated rule.[32]

Pope Leo XIII, after having received the petition of the South American Bishops for the celebration of a plenary council, left it to them to choose the place of meeting.[33] The exact place, there-

---

[28] Chelodi, *Ius de Personis,* p. 374; Decr. Sacrae Congregationis Consistorialis, 15 febr. 1919—*AAS,* XI (1919), 72; 175.

[29] Chelodi, *op cit.,* p. 374, nota 5.

[30] Cance-Arquer, *El Código de Decrecho Canónico* (2 vols., Barcelona, 1934), I, 200 (hereafter cited as *El Código*).

[31] Canon 338, § 3.

[32] Canon 338, § 3.

[33] Augustine, *A Commentary on the New Code of Canon Law* (8 vols.,

fore, for the celebration of the council is, in the law, left undetermined. The determining of it rests with the judgment of the Roman Pontiff or his Legate, but the convenience of all concerned should be the deciding factor.

Article 2. Convocation of the Council

A. Provision of the Code

Canon 281.—Ordinarii plurium provinciarum ecclesiasticarum in Concilium plenarium convenire possunt, petita tamen venia a Romano Pontifice, qui suum Legatum designat ad Concilium convocandum eique praesidendum.

Aside from the Cardinals, the Roman Curia, the Legates of the Roman Pontiff and the Metropolitans, the particular councils also have a participation in the supreme legislative power derived from the ecclesiastical law. During the formation of the present Code of Canon Law these councils were of great efficacy.[34] After the time of the Apostles until the end of the second century there were no evident traces of the existence of such councils. It is supposed that the first particular council was celebrated in Rome about the year 196, during the reign of Septimius Severus Augustus, by Pope St. Victor I.[35] The practice of holding particular councils year by year was introduced from the sixth century onward,[36] and from the year 1425, when Pope Martin V approved in part the canons of the Council of Constance, particular councils were to be held every three years.[37] Provincial councils were convoked by the

---

2. ed., St. Louis and London, 1918-1924), II, 298 (hereafter cited as *A Commentary*).

[34] Toso, *Commentaria Minora,* III, 103.

[35] Thomassinus, *Vetus et Nova Disciplina,* Pars II, lib. III, cap. 45, p. 343.

[36] Lib. I, Ep. 1; Lib. III, Ep. 57; Lib. IX, Ep. 222—*MGH, Registrum,* Vol. I, pars I, pp. 1-2 and pp. 216-217; Vol. II, pars I, pp. 213-214. Cf. Murphy, *Legislative Powers of the Provincial Council,* The Catholic University of America Canon Law Studies, n. 257 (Washington, D. C.: The Catholic University of America Press, 1948), p. 7 (hereafter cited as *Legislative Powers*).

[37] Wernz, *Ius Decretalium,* II, n. 853; Hinschius, *Das Kirchenrecht,* III, 502-509; Hefele-Leclercq, *Histoire,* VII, 410.

Metropolitans, and the plenary councils generally by the Patriarchs and Primates, but every once in a while the temporal rulers would take it upon themselves to call for a plenary council.[38]

The present law no longer retains the ancient practice which gave the right of convoking plenary councils to Patriarchs, Exarchs or Primates.[39] The obligation of informing the members to be summoned of the convocation and the summoning of them to the council belongs only to the Apostolic Legate appointed by the Pope for this purpose.[40] The Apostolic Legate alone can licitly convoke the plenary council after receiving his designation as the representative of the Holy Father, and for this reason he must make the convocation personally. A legitimate convocation therefore is needed, because otherwise it would be wanting in juridical authority.[41]

By general law the title of patriarch in the Latin rite does not confer any special jurisdiction.[42] The prerogatives of honor and precedence alone belong to it.[43] This special prerogative of honor due to the patriarchs is based on custom and ancient tradition.[44] The Latin term "primate" is equivalent to the name "exarch." This word appeared in the I Council of Constantinople (381), and again in the Council of Chalcedone (451). In the Latin Church

---

[38] Hefele-Leclercq, *Histoire,* VI, 975 ff.; 986 ff.; Hinschius, *Das Kirchenrecht,* III, 578 ff.; Wernz, *Ius Decretalium,* II, n. 853.

[39] V.g., The Bishop of Carthage convoked the Councils of Africa, the Primate of Toledo those of Spain, the Primate of Arles those of Southern Gaul—Thomassinus, *Vetus et Nova Disciplina,* Pars I, lib. I, cap. 38, p. 230.

[40] Ayrinhac, *Constitution of the Church in the New Code of Canon Law* (New York: Blase Benziger and Company, Inc., 1925) p. 104, n. 81 (hereafter cited as *Constitution of the Church*).

[41] Toso, *Commentaria Minora,* III, 104.

[42] Canon 271.

[43] Cfr. canon 280.

[44] In the I Council of Constantinople (381) the Oriental Bishops conceded to the Bishops of Constantinople the place of honor immediately after the Roman Pontiff for the reason that Constantinople was the New Rome. Though the Pope did not for many centuries admit this ruling of the Council of Constantinople, the bishops of that city actually obtained, soon after the council was held, the jurisdiction of an exarch over all the province of Thrace and over Asia Minor and Pontus.

the title of primate does not confer any special jurisdiction; it also is but a title of honor.[45] In some countries of the Western Church this primatial dignity was claimed by several bishops. This is why each country has at least one primate, though sometimes several. Although some of the primates have jurisdiction conjointly with their primatial dignity,[46] this does not mean that they have the right to convoke any plenary council without the permission of the Holy See.[47] The rights of the primates can be traced not so much to ancient custom as to special concessions made by the Holy See.

The present discipline teaches also that no metropolitan has superior authority over other metropolitans, but that all metropolitans are equal and are immediately subject to the Holy See. The Code itself gives the power of jurisdiction to the metropolitans, but nowhere can it be found that they can convoke a plenary council without the permission of the Holy See.[48]

B. Permission Required for the Celebration

Although plenary councils are permitted in general by the Code, nevertheless the permission of the Pope is necessary for the celebration.[49] Inasmuch as the word *plenarium* does not specifically determine the number of provinces needed to form a plenary council, the special instructions of the Holy See specify which ecclesiastical provinces are to participate in the plenary council, when one is to be celebrated.[50] The Church has always been wary of granting indiscriminately permission for the celebration of plenary councils. Much depends upon conditions and the state of affairs in the nations whence come the requests for such a permission. Permission to celebrate a plenary council was denied by Rome to

---

[45] Canon 271.

[46] V.g., The Primate of Esztergom in Hungary has a certain primatial authority.

[47] Nilles, *Commentaria,* pp. 16, 19 ff.; Bouix, *Concilio Provinciali,* pp. 12 ff.

[48] Canons 272-275.

[49] Canon 281.

[50] Coronata, *Institutiones,* I, p. 431, n. 5; Wernz, *Ius Decretalium,* II, n. 855; Chelodi, *Ius de Personis,* p. 374; Wernz-Vidal, *Ius Canonicum,* II, 676.

the Bishops of France and Germany in the nineteenth century.[51] The same permission, however, was later granted to the Bishops of America, Ireland and Australia. In recent years the Holy See has been generous in granting such permission.[52]

C. Presiding Officer

The ordinaries of several ecclesiastical provinces may meet in a plenary council, but they must ask first the permission of the Holy See, which will appoint a legate to preside over the council.[53] The president has full power to determine the manner of proceeding. Even though a plenary council is convoked by the head of a nation, the presidency of it resides in the legate of the Roman Pontiff. The different meetings held in a plenary council are not legitimate if not presided over by a delegate from the Apostolic See.[54]

In regard to the person who convokes and presides over the council, there is a great distinction between provincial and plenary councils. Canon 281[55] clearly states that the papal legate presides over the plenary council. In this capacity the papal legate is by no means a simply *"primus inter pares."* He determines the order which is to be followed. He opens the council, transfers it, if necessary, prorogues and closes it.[56] Inasmuch as the Apostolic Legate performs the functions of his office in the name of the Holy Father,[57] and according to the tenor of the mandate and of the law has a true jurisdiction, i.e., ranks in power above everybody in the council,[58] the consent of the Fathers is not needed to transfer, prorogue or close a plenary council.

---

[51] *Coll. Lac.*, IV, 3 ff.; V, 994 ff.; 1336 ff.

[52] V.g., to the Latin American Bishops in 1899; for the celebration of the I Plenary Council of Quebec in 1909; to the Chinese Hierarchy in 1924; to the Bishops of India in 1950, and to the hierarchy of the Philippine Islands in 1953.

[53] Canon 281.

[54] Toso, *Commentaria Minora*, III, 104.

[55] *". . . eique presidendum."*

[56] Canon 288.

[57] Toso, *op. cit.*, III, 109.

[58] Coronata, *Institutiones*, p. 431.

Article 3. Members of the Council with Deliberative Vote[59]

A. Deliberative Vote Granted by Law

Canon 282.—§ 1.—Concilio plenario assistere debent cum suffragio deliberativo, praeter Legatum Apostolicum, Metropolitae, Episcopi residentiales, qui sui loco, mittere possunt Coadjutorem vel Auxiliarem, Apostolici dioecesium Administratores, Abbates vel Paelati nullius, Vicarii Apostolici, praefecti Apostolici, Vicarii Capitulares.

The convocation by the appointed legate must be sent to all those who are obliged to attend the council. In the plenary council the following persons having a deliberative vote should be present: the Papal Legate, the Archbishops, the residential Bishops, who may send their Coadjutor or Auxiliary Bishops to take their place, the Apostolic Administrators of dioceses,[60] the Abbots and Prelates *nullius,* Vicars and Prefects Apostolic,[61] and Vicars Capitular.[62] Persons, therefore, who have ordinary powers of jurisdiction in the territory which is subject to the conciliar decrees enjoy a deliberative vote at plenary councils.[63]

1. Local Ordinaries

Prelates who exercise ordinary jurisdiction over a territory in both the internal and external forum are called local ordinaries.[64]

---

[59] One has a deliberative vote in an assembly when the ballot that is taken is counted in the reaching of some definitive conclusion, otherwise it is consultative.—Cf. Wagner, *Dictionnaire de Droit Canonique* (5. ed., 4 vols., Paris, 1901), III, 716 (hereafter cited as *Dictionnaire*).

[60] Canon 312.—Dioecesis canonice erectae regimen, sive plena, sive vacante sede, aliquando Summus Pontifex ob graves et speciales causas administratori Apostolico vel in perpetuum vel ad tempus committit.

[61] "Vicarii et praefecti Apostolici sunt Praelati ecclesiastici a Sede Apostolica nominati, qui in regione ubi hierarchia nunquam exstitit, vel nondum restituta est, vel inchoatum aliquid adhuc secumfert, ad munia apostolica sub auctoritate S. C. de Prop. Fide exercenda, vices S. Pontificis agunt."—De Meester, *Juris Canonici et Juris Canonico-Civilis Compendium* (3 vols. in 4, ed. nova, Brugis: Sumptibus et Typis Societatis Sancti Augustini, 1921-1928), II, 120 (hereafter cited as *Compendium*).

[62] A vicar capitular is the local ordinary of a territory, *sede vel abbatia vel praelatura vacante*—cf. Wernz-Vidal, *Ius Canonicum,* II, 899-990; The Vicar Capitular is elected by the *Capitulum.*—Cf. canon 432, §§ 1, 3.

[63] Cf. canon 282, § 1.

[64] Cf. canon 197, § 2.

Their jurisdiction extends, primarily and directly, over a territory; secondarily, it has reference to the persons residing in the territory. They are distinguished from religious ordinaries, whose jurisdiction directly applies to persons, and not to a place.[65] The vicars general of those ordinaries are not included in the list mentioned in canon 282, § 1, because a vicar general is just an *alter ego,* and thus the exercise of his power of jurisdiction depends upon the will of his proper odrinary.[66] This is the reason why the said canon does not give an equal right to the vicars general with their bishops in deciding conciliar matters.

The jurisdiction of the local ordinaries arises with the taking of canonical possession of their office. The taking of possession of an office consists ordinarily in the presentation of the Apostolic letters of appointment, which can be made either by the person appointed, or by a proxy, when duly authorized and determined by the appointed person,[67] to the proper authority of the territory as specified by law.[68] The right of local ordinaries to be members of the council is determined not simply by the reception of the episcopal consecration but mostly by the possession of local jurisdiction.[69] Bishops, therefore, who have taken the canonical possession of their office, though they have not yet been consecrated, must be invited as full members of the conciliar assembly. This rule is also applied to other local ordinaries who are not bishops at all.

Obviously, any local ordinary who exercises full jurisdiction over a territory which is subject to the conciliar decrees is included among the members of the conciliar assembly with the exception of course of the vicars general. Are the pro-vicars and pro-

---

[65] Wernz-Vidal, *Ius Canonicum,* II, 427.

[66] Wernz-Vidal, *Ius Canonicum,* II, 690-691; canons 294, § 1, and 323, § 3, indicate the appointment of vicars general in ecclesiastical territories, while canon 366, § 1, shows that ordinarily a diocese should have at least one vicar general.

[67] Canon 1445.—Possessio beneficii, etiam per procuratorem, speciale mandatum habentem, capi potest.

[68] Cf. canons 293, § 1; 313; 322, § 1; 334, § 3; and 353.

[69] Conc. Trident. sess. XXIV, *de ref.,* c. 2; Nilles, *Commentaria,* p. 68; Fagnanus, *Commentaria,* Lib. V, tit. 1, cap. 25, n. 28, p. 25.

prefects apostolic also excluded? No, because when the vicar or prefect dies or cannot exercise his jurisdiction, the pro-vicar or pro-prefect, as the case may be, immediately assumes the entire government of the territory and continues in it until the Holy See fills the vacancy.[70] In other words they are to act as administrators as they are constituted local ordinaries by law.[71] However, unlike a temporary apostolic administrator, according to canon 310, § 2, they have all the faculties of the vicar or prefect. Therefore during the interim of the vacancy they have the right to be included among the members of the conciliar assembly like the vicar or prefect apostolic.

The apostolic administrator who is constituted a local ordinary in a diocese, whether *sede plena* or *sede vacante*,[72] has also a deliberative vote. Thus a priest who is constituted a local ordinary when the see or any equivalent territorial jurisdiction is merely impeded, i.e., when the original jurisdiction of the prelate has not been terminated, but simply has been rendered incapable of being exercised,[73] can attend the plenary council with a deliberative vote, because such representation of the territory in the council can only be exercised by this administrator.

Vicars Capitular are constituted in office only when the see is vacant, i.e., when the original jurisdiction of the prelate has been terminated by the vacancy of the see.[74] As local ordinaries, therefore, they do have the right to a deliberative vote.

With the exception of Abbots and Prelates *nullius*, religious are not included among those who must be invited to attend with deliberative vote. Augustine (1872-1943), wondering why superiors general of exempt clerical institutes and abbots presiding over

[70] Cf. Winslow, *Vicars and Prefects Apostolic*, The Catholic University of America Canon Law Studies, n. 24 (Washington, D. C.: The Catholic University of America, 1924), p. 65; Coleman, *The Minister of Confirmation*, The Catholic University of America Canon Law Studies, n. 125 (Washington, D. C.: The Catholic University of America Press, 1941), pp. 14, 122.

[71] Canons 309, § 2, and 310.

[72] Cf. Canon 312.

[73] Cf. canons 309, §§ 2 & 4; 217; 327, § 2; 429, § 1.

[74] Cf. canon 432, § 1.

monastic congregations are excluded from the right of attending a plenary council, said: "We are at a loss to find a solid reason for the exclusion of the aforesaid superiors from the right of assisting at a plenary council, the more so since Cardinal Gasparri gives no text for this enactment. But where there is no right, there is no obligation (to attend), although an invitation might be tendered."[75] Coronata, however, holds that the plenary council is concerned with matters which directly affect the people, whose spiritual well-being belongs *per se* not to the religious but to the secular clergy, and observes also that a major religious superior would be acting imprudently if he refused to attend a plenary council when the Apostolic Legate has invited him.[76]

Canon 282, § 1, includes residential bishops among those who must attend plenary councils, and states that they will have the right to a deliberative vote in its resolutions. It makes it clear also that if the residential bishop does not attend but wishes to be represented then his coadjutor, if he has one, is to be his representative. In view of canon 351, § 3,[77] it appears that the coadjutor not only may, but has the right, other things being equal, to be appointed the proxy for the residential bishop. Coadjutor bishops, who possess full powers of diocesan administration, i.e., who rule a diocese with full jurisdiction over a territory which is subject to the conciliar decrees, are included among the members who hold the right of a deliberative vote,[78] for the simple reason that such coadjutor bishops seem to be at least not inferior in office to apostolic administrators.[79]

---

[75] *A Commentary,* II, 299.

[76] *Institutiones, I,* p. 430, footnote 7; Beste; *Introductio,* p. 257; Cocchi, *Commentarium in Codicem Iuris Canonici* (8 vols. in 5, Vols. III & VI, 3. ed. recognita, Taurinorum Augustae: Marietti, 1931 & 1933), III, n. 221 (hereafter cited as *Commentarium*).

[77] "Quae Coadjutor potest et vult exercere, Episcopus habitualiter alii ne deleget."

[78] Wernz-Vidal, *Ius Canonicum,* II, 676; Vermeersch-Creusen, *Epitome,* II, 313.

[79] Cf. Lynch, *Coadjutors and Auxiliaries of Bishops,* The Catholic University of America Canon Law Studies, n. 238 (Washington, D. C.: The Catholic University of America Press, 1947), pp. 75-76.

2. Procurators

The Code has no provisions on the qualifications of procurators, but the Congregation of the Council as far back as 1638 decreed that it is sufficient that they be, *"habiles, doctores, et discreti."*[80]

A residential bishop who has a coadjutor or auxiliary and is personally impeded from attending the council can send his coadjutor or auxiliary bishop in his own place and with the privilege of a deliberative vote.[81] The force of the law on conciliar membership seems to mean that each territory which is recognized by the Holy See as a constituent subject of a conciliar decree should have its ordinary as a personal representative, i.e., a voting member in the council. This is the reason why a coadjutor or auxiliary bishop, when he acts as a proxy for his bishop, has a deliberative vote. The coadjutor or auxiliary bishop is the only procurator in a plenary council who has a deliberative vote granted by law.

The procurator should have a special written mandate to act for his bishop,[82] while the latter, i.e. the bishop, must send to the President of the council a letter stating the existence of a just impediment for his absence, with the corresponding reasons and proofs that would convince a prudent man, v. g., the handicap of ill-health, the burden of advancing years, etc.

B. Deliberative Vote Accorded by Authority

Titular bishops residing in the territory where the plenary council is held have no right from the common law to be present at such a council, but the Legate may be instructed to demand their attendance, and in that case, unless the contrary is stated in the summons, their vote is deliberative.[83] The question of residence is to be determined by the domicile or quasi-domicile one has within

[80] S. C. C., *Tarraconen.*, 4 dec. 1638—*Fontes,* n. 2596.

[81] Canon 282, § 1.

[82] Cf. canon 1659, § 1: Petra. *Commentaria ad Constitutiones Apostolicas* (5 vols. in 2, Venetiis, 1729), I, p. 279, n. 39 (hereafter cited as *Commentaria*).

[83] Canon 282, § 2: Etiam Episcopi titulares, in territorio degentes, si a Legato Pontificio, secundum receptas instructiones, ad Concilium vocentur, adesse debent habentque suffragium deliberativum, nisi in convocatione aliud expresse caveatur.

the limits of the territory.[84] The Apostolic Legate cannot summon the titular bishops to the plenary council, or also by his own will grant to them at the same time the right of a deliberative vote; he must have an instruction from the Pope to do so.[85] The right of the titular bishops to cast a deliberative vote during the deliberation in the council is a privilege granted to them. Though they may be invited to the council with the right of a deliberative vote, yet they cannot send any procurator,[86] for their invitation is not based on the law itself, since it is simply a personal concession of the Apostolic Legate to them as individuals. Thus they cannot extend their right to another person, who then might serve as their procurator.

Article 4. Persons in the Plenary Council with Consultative Vote

A. Members of the Clergy, Secular and Religious

Canon 282.—§ 3. Alii ex utroque clero viri, forte ad Concilium invitati, suffragio non gaudent nisi consultivo.

The Apostolic Legate has full liberty in inviting other members of the clergy, whether religious or secular, who, however, have only a consultative vote.[87] These priests will serve as theologians and canonists, or will discharge the various offices of the council, v. g., promoter, secretary and notaries.[88] It has been a common practice that each prelate be accompanied by one or two theologians or canonists, who act as his personal advisers.[89] The invited members of the clergy are not obliged to send a representative if they cannot attend the council personally.

---

[84] Cf. canon 92; Vermeersch-Creusen, *Epitome,* I, 313.

[85] Blat, *Commentarium Textus Codicis Iuris Canonici* (5 vols. in 6, Romae, 1919-1927; Vol. II, *De Personis* (1919); Vol. III, Partes II-VI, 1923), II, p. 299, n. 290 (hereafter cited as *Commentarium*).

[86] Coronata, *Institutiones,* I, 426.

[87] Cf. canon 282, § 3; Vermeersch-Creusen, *Epitome,* 312.

[88] Bargilliat, *Praelectiones Iuris Canonici* (28. ed., ab auctore recognita et recentioribus decretis accommodata, 2 vols., Parisiis, 1913), I, n. 680 (hereafter cited as *Praelectiones*).

[89] Ojetti, *Synopsis Rerum Moralium et Iuris Pontificii* (2 vols. in 1, 2. ed., emendata et aucta, Prati, 1904-1905), p. 402 (hereafter cited as *Synopsis*).

B. Procurators.

Canon 287.—§ 1. Qui Concilio plenario aut provinciali interesse debent cum voto deliberativo, si iusto impedimento detineantur, mittant procuratorem et impedimentum probent.

§ 2. Procurator, si fuerit unus ex Patribus quibus est votum deliberativum, duplici voto non gaudet; si non fuerit, habet votum dumtaxat consultivum.

At present the practice of sending proxies is not favored by the Code. The above quoted canon in its first and second paragraphs not only requires that a just impediment be proved, when the principal invitee is unable to attend the council, but that procurators as such shall not have any deliberative vote. It seems that the obligation of sending a procurator does not rest on titular bishops. It is applied to only those who have the right of a deliberative vote as granted by law and upon whom the obligation of personal attendance is imposed.

The procurator must have a special written mandate of his bishop stating that the procurator will act in the bishop's place.[90] The bishop should also address to the President of the council a letter certifying the legitimate reasons for his absence.[91] Sickness is a legitimate and generally the principal impediment to one's presence at the council, but it excuses only while it lasts.[92]

In the selection of procurators, anyone among the Fathers of the council can be chosen to act as proxy for another member who may be impeded from coming. The proxy, if he be one of the Fathers who has a deliberative vote, shall not, however, have a double vote,[93] i.e., he does not possess an additional vote as the representative of an absent bishop. This norm is also applied when a temporary apostolic administrator of a certain diocese is at the same time the residential bishop of another diocese.[94]

---

[90] Cf. canon 1659, § 1; Petra, *Commentaria,* I, p. 279, n. 39.

[91] Cf. canon 287; § 1; S. C. C., *Tarraconen.,* 4 dec. 1638—*Fontes,* n. 2596; Blat, *Commentarium,* II, p. 303, n. 298.

[92] Cance-Arquer, *El Codigo,* I, 202.

[93] Canon 287, § 2.

[94] McDonough, *Apostolic Administrators,* The Catholic University of America Canon Law Studies, n. 139 (Washington, D. C.: The Catholic University of America Press, 1941), pp. 132-134.

If coadjutor bishops are convoked to a plenary council, they have a deliberative vote unless the convocation states the contrary. If the coadjutor is sent as the representative of the principal bishop, he will likewise have the right to a deliberative vote.[95] There would be no reason for the clause about Coadjutors and Auxiliaries of Bishops in canon 282, § 1, if they do not have a deliberative vote as proxy. For it is evident from canon 287, § 2, that any proxy has at least a consultative vote. Therefore it is to be concluded that canon 282, § 1, is an exception to the general rule of canon 287, § 2.

In general, of course, the persons selected as procurators must be suited to the work of giving advice to the conciliar body, and must be well informed about the situation of the diocese. They must be well recommended for their prudence, and should be doctors in canon law or theology, or at least well versed in these matters.[96]

The procurator in the plenary council has only a consultative vote, unless he already enjoys the right of a deliberative vote.[97] The word *dumtaxat* of the clause *habet votum dumtaxat consultivum* is very important, because it shows the difference between the former and the present law. The former permitted a deliberative vote to the procurator of the absent members of the council with the approval of the Fathers of the council.[98] The basis for this difference in the present law is the desire of the Church that the chief pastors of the flock be present personally at the council.

Article 5. Obligation of Attendance

A. Who must be Present

In the early Church, when councils were frequently held and the means of travel were undeveloped, it is understandable that

[95] Canon, 282, § 1.

[96] S.C.C., *Tarraconen.*, 4 dec. 1638: "Procuratores sint habiles, doctores, et discreti."—*Fontes*, n. 2596.

[97] Canon 287, § 2.

[98] Decree 60 of the II Plenary Council of Baltimore (1866) provided that all procurators of the absent Fathers were to be given a deliberative vote—*Coll. Lac.*, III, 417. But this provision, as contrary to canon 287, § 2, is abrogated by the Code. Cf. canon 6, 2°.

there would have been some laxity in the matter of attendance. In the fourth century, bishops were reminded of their obligation to attend promptly or to send a representative in the case of unavoidable absence. "A sufficiently grave necessity" was the excuse admitted by the IV Council of Carthage (938), with the additional clause that the impeded bishop in such a case was to send a procurator to take his place at the council.[99] The ruling of the subsequent council of Carthage (401) was more explicit, when it stated that the absent bishop was to explain by letter the cause of his absence.[100] Commentators on the *Decretum Gratiani* (ca. 1140) stated that this excuse could be delivered through a messenger. The pertinent canons of the above mentioned Councils of Carthage are cited as sources of the present law on attendance as embodied in paragraph one of canon 287. Thus members who have a deliberative vote accorded to them by law must attend the council,[101] and if they are impeded from coming in person, they shall send a procurator and prove the impediment.[102] It has been shown in the preceding articles that the procurator does not have any deliberative vote in the council, except when he is a coadjutor or auxiliary bishop representing his own bishop. This denial of the deliberative vote to procurators manifests the will of the legislator that the members should be personally present at the council whenever possible.[103] The words *mittere possint* of canon 282, § 2, therefore, mean to say that residential bishops cannot send their coadjutor or auxiliary bishops as their procurators to the council whenever they can themselves be present in person.

Titular bishops are also obliged to be present in the council. The law itself determines this obligation.[104] In summary, therefore, only those who under the law must be invited to the plenary council

---

[99] Can. 2—Bruns, I, 43; c. 9, D. XVIII.

[100] C. 10, D. XVIII; cf. *Glossa ordinaria,* ad c. 10, D. XVIII, s. v. *litteratorie.*

[101] Cf. canon 282, § 1: . . . assistere debent . . .

[102] Canon 287, § 1.—Qui Concilio plenario aut provinciali interesse debent cum voto deliberativo, si iusto impedimento detineantur, mittant procuratorum et impedimentum probent.

[103] Cf. supra, articles 3 and 4.

[104] Canon 282, § 2.

have the strict obligation to attend it. The obligation of attending the council is clearly manifested in the law.[105]

B. Premature Departure

It is clear that the deliberations of the council would be jeopardized if the members of the council were free to leave at any time and for any reason which they themselves might think sufficient. The law of the Church has never been sympathetic with such a procedure. The II Council of Arles (433-552) enacted severe punishment for deserters.[106] Moreover, the Code has a clear prohibition against any departure, except when it is made because of a just cause, and always with the consent of the President of the council.[107] Canon 289 is similar to canon 225, which contains provisions for ecumenical councils. In canon 289 only those who received an invitation to attend are obliged by the rule.

As the President is the one responsible for the observance of good order, it might seem that rulings on premature departure are unnecessary. Unhappily these rights and prerogatives of the President have not always been taken for granted. Once the council is opened, therefore, all its necessary members, i.e., those who are obliged to attend it, whether with deliberative or consultative vote, must remain to the end. If by necessity one is obliged to leave before the close, the permission must be obtained from the Apostolic Legate.

Article 6. Precedence

A. Its Necessity

In every well organized society there must be a rule to be followed and an order to be fulfilled so that everybody will know the norm of conduct he has to observe and the place he has to occupy. In this way, honor will be given to whom it is due, and thus unnecessary disputes will be avoided.

---

[105] Canon 282, § 1: . . . assistere debent . . .; canon 282, § 2: . . . adesse debent . . . ; canon 287, § 1: . . . interesse debent . . . ; canon 389, § 1: . . . interesse debent. . . .

[106] C. 12, D. XVIII.

[107] Canon 289.

Precedence[108] signifies the right to a specified place of honor in public gatherings, functions, processions, and the like,[109] before other persons. It is determined according to the general principles contained in canon 106, which, however, are sometimes modified by special norms. Thus, the precedence of persons attached to the Pontifical Household is to be regulated in accordance with the special rules and traditions of the Papal Palace.[110] Their privileges, moreover, have been revised and are now governed exclusively by the Apostolic Constitution, *Ad incrementum,* of August 15, 1934.[111]

B. Norms of Precedence at the Plenary Council

The question of precedence sometimes gives rise to controversies. In canon law the general rule of precedence is determined with a view to the rank of the person represented.[112] Thus, an apostolic legate, provided he be a cardinal, precedes all others.[113] A principle of distinction is vested in the rank one holds. Rank denotes the relevant degree of jurisdiction, of office, and dignity, but not that of holy orders,[114] for the order to which one has been raised is identical with the ordination one has received among the various degrees of the hierarchy of orders.[115] Persons, therefore, who belong to a higher rank precede those of an inferior rank, and persons of the same rank but of a different order have precedence according to the higher or inferior order.[116] Thus, the Cardinals, who always have precedence over all other dignitaries, except the

---

[108] The term comes from the Latin word *praecedere,* which means to go before another.

[109] Abbo-Hannan, *The Sacred Canons,* I, 155.

[110] Canon 106, 7°; *AAS,* XXVI (1934), 497.

[111] *AAS,* XXVI (1934), 497.

[112] Canon 106, 1°; Vito, *Note Canoniche sulla Precedenza* (Verona, 1924), p. 13 (hereafter cited as *Sulla Precedenza.*)

[113] Canon 239, § 1, n. 21. *Ordo in Concilio Plenario Servandus* (Typis Polyglottis Vaticanis, 1946), p. 11 (hereafter cited as *Ordo Servandus*).

[114] Abbo-Hannan, *The Sacred Canons,* I, 156; Beste, *Introductio,* 165; Coronata, *Institutiones,* I, p. 188; Vito, *op. cit.,* p. 9. nota 1.

[115] Woywod-Smith, *A Practical Commentary on the Code of Canon Law* (revised ed., London: B. Herder, 1952), p. 57 (herefater cited as *Practical Commentary*).

[116] Cf. canon 106, 3°.

Apostolic Legate, as stated before, rank according as they are Cardinal bishops, priests, or deacons, and they are followed by the patriarchs, the residential archbishops and residential bishops.[117] The titular archbishops and titular bishops, who have no "authority," properly or specifically at the council, follow the latter.

To avoid needless unpleasant contentions among the ones present at the plenary council who are of the same rank and of the same order, the Code rules that the one who was promoted earlier precedes the one whose promotion occurred later. The word "promotion" here means the preconization (made in the consistory) or nomination (made outside the consistory) to the episcopacy,[118] and not the date of the promotion or accession to a given suffragan see.[119] If two prelates are of equal rank, order, and promotion, the date of their ordination is to be ascertained. According to canon 950[120] the term ordination includes the conferring of the tonsure. So when two prelates received the first tonsure, were elevated to the priesthood, and promoted to the episcopacy on the same date, but one between them received the sacerdotal ordination from the Roman Pontiff, then this prelate ordained by the Roman Pontiff precedes the other.[121] The words "Roman Pontiff" are to be interpreted strictly. Thus, an ordination performed by the Cardinal

---

117 This rule was observed at the Vatican Council—Cf. Cranderath-Kirch, *Geschichte des Vatikanischen Konzils von seiner ersten Ankündigung bis zu seiner Vertagung* (3 vols., Freiburg im Breisgau, 1903-1906), I, 392.

118 Cf. S. R. C., *Iaren.*, 15 apr. 1904—*Decreta Authentica Congregationis Sacorum Rituum* (5 vols., Romae: Ex typographia Polyglotta, 1898-1901. Appendix I, 1912; Appendix II, 1927), n. 4133 (hereafter cited as *Decr. Auth. S. R. C.*); S. R. C., *Terulen.*, 20 nov. 1677—*Decr. Auth. S. R. C.*, n. 1606; S.R.C., *Segobricen.*, 21 mart. 1909—*Decr. Auth.* S.R.C., n 270. Cf. also *Periodica de Re Morali, Canonica, Liturgica,* XIV (1925), 180-182 (hereafter cited as *Periodica*).

119 Cf. Resp., Pontificia Commissio Interpretationis (hereafter cited as P. C. I.), 10 nov. 1925, ad II—*AAS,* XVII (1925), 582. Cf. also *Periodica,* XIV (1925), 181.

120 "In iure verba: ordinare . . . ordinatio . . . comprehendunt et ipsam primam tonsuram . . ."

121 Cf. Santi-Leitner, *Praelectiones Juris Canonici* (5 vols. in 3, 4. ed., Ratisbonae, 1903-1905), I, 369 (hereafter cited as *Praelectiones*).

Vicar of Rome, or by another Cardinal, does not involve the said privilege, but if one is delegated specially by the Pope to ordain a cleric in his name, it would have the same effect as an ordination performed by the Pontiff himself.[122] If in rank, order, promotion, and time of ordination some members are still equal, then the natural age must be the one to be considered.[123]

One who acts in place of another properly receives his precedence from that other person, but those who are present at councils and other similar meetings as procurators take their places after those of the same rank who are present in their own name.[124] Thus the procurator of an archbishop takes place after all the archbishops who are present in their own right, but before all the bishops, though the archbishop whose place he is taking has the right to precede the other archbishops in view of the seniority of his promotion.[125]

Latin and Oriental bishops or priests are equal, *ceteris paribus*.[126] The above-mentioned norms and other particular rules of precedence mentioned in the Code[127] are to be observed in the plenary council during the processions,[128] in the seating and voting, and with regard to the subscribing of the acts.[129] If in spite of the above-mentioned rules a controversy over precedence in plenary councils arises, it would seem, as there is no specified law in the Code regarding such a question, that the one who has authority to decide it is the President or Apostolic Legate of the said council.

---

[122] Augustine, *A Commentary,* II, 39.

[123] Vito, *Sulla Precedenza,* p. 10.

[124] Canon 106, 1°; Vito, *Sulla Precedenza,* p. 13.

[125] Beste, *Introductio,* p. 165; Vito, *loc. cit.*

[126] Canon 106, 4°; Vito, *op. cit.,* p. 11, in notis.

[127] V.g., in canons 269, § 2; 271, and 280.

[128] Cf. Moretti, *Ceremoniale iuxta Ritum Romanum, seu de Sacris Functionibus Episcopo Celebrante, Assistente, Absente* (4 vols., Taurini: Marietti, 1936-1939), III, nn. 2508, 2515 (hereafter cited as *Coeremoniale*).

[129] Cocchi, *Commentarium,* III, 135.

Article 7. Profession of Faith

A. The Obligation of the Profession of Faith

At the opening of the plenary council the profession of faith is prescribed.[130] One does not satisfy the obligation of making the profession of faith when one acts through a representative or before a layman.[131] It is a general principle of law that one may appoint a delegate or substitute to do things which one has a right to do or is obliged to do by law; but there are exceptions, and this is one of them, in which the law requires a personal performance. Thus, the President or Apostolic Legate cannot permit that one who would be assisting the council in person would make the profession of faith by procurator, even when the said procurator has a special mandate from his principal. The Code expressly states that any custom that is expressly reprobated in the law of the Code is not reasonable,[132] and since there is such an express reprobation in canon 1408,[133] every contrary custom that now exists or had existed, though it be an immemorial one, whether universal or particular, is abrogated. The emergence of a future custom against the law of making the profession of faith is rendered impossible.[134] The reason why the obligation of making the profession of faith cannot be satisfied before a layman lies in the fact that a mere layman lacks spiritual and juridical power to receive a profession of faith, which is in itself a jurisdictional act.[135]

The Code allows those who attend a council with either a deliberative or consultative vote to make their profession of faith either before the presiding officer or his delegate. This delegate may be any member of the assembly.[136] It is not necessary that all who are bound to make the profession of faith do so individually. One

---

[130] Canon 1406.

[131] Canon 1407; Blat, *Commentarium,* III, pars IV, p. 371, nn. 297 sq.; Coronata, *Institutiones,* II, p. 359, n. 968.

[132] Canon 27, § 2:—Consuetudo quae in iure expresse reprobantur, non est rationabilis.

[133] "Reprobatur quaelibet consuetudo contra canones huius tituli."

[134] Cf. Augustine, *A Commentary,* VI, 490, 382.

[135] Cf. Augustine, *A Commentary,* VI, 490, 382; Blat, *Commentarium,* III, pars IV, p. 428, n. 344; Coronata, *Institutiones,* II, p. 359, n. 968, 1°.

[136] Cf. S. C. Consist., 25 oct. 1910, ad VIII—*AAS,* II (1910), 857; Coronata, *Institutiones,* II, p. 359, n. 968. Cf. also *Ordo Servandus,* p. 44.

may read the formula, the others repeating it phrase by phrase after him, or one may read the entire formula or profession orally, and then each one may separately signify his assent under oath by way of a shorter formula.[137] The profession of faith is to be made first by the members of the council in the presence of its president or his delegate, and then by the president in the presence of the entire council. It takes place immediately after the reading of the preliminary decrees in the first session.[138]

Although this grave obligation regarding the profession of faith rests principally on the superior before whom it is to be made,[139] nevertheless it also binds those who are obliged to make it or take it. If they fail to obey, they should be reminded of their duty. Anyone who contumaciously refuses to perform this act is liable to the penalties stated by the Code, even to the extent of depriving him of the right to take part in the council.[140]

B. Persons Obliged to Make the Profession of Faith

Documents of the seventh century testify that a public profession of faith was made by the Roman Pontiff on the occasion of his election to the papacy, or of his coronation.[141] The Pope himself used to send a kind of public profession to the Patriarchs of the East soon after his accession to the Papal throne.[142] The profession of faith was generally connected with the oath of obedience, which was imposed on the prelates, and especially on those persons who were immediately subject to the Holy See.[143] The present discipline regarding this act was essentially enacted by the Council of Trent. Later on, decrees of Pius IV (1559-1565) specified more

---

[137] S. C. Consist., 25 oct. 1910, ad IV—*AAS,* II (1910), 856; Coronata, *Institutiones,* II, p. 361; Wernz, *Ius Decretalium,* III, n. 19; Bouscaren, *Canon Law,* p. 793; Ayrinhac, *Administrative Legislation in the New Code of Canon Law* (New York: Longmans, Green and Company, 1930), pp. 305, 306.

[138] Canon 1406, § 1, n. 1; Moretti, *Coeremoniale,* III, n. 2468.

[139] Vermeersch-Creusen, *Epitome,* II, n. 739; Cocchi, *Commentarium,* VI, 179.

[140] Canon 2403; De Meester, *Compendium,* III, pars. I, n. 1389.

[141] Wernz, *Ius Decretalium,* III, 15 ff.

[142] *MGH, Registrum,* I, 5, 28, 39, 438, 448.

[143] C. 4, X, *de electione et electi potestate,* I, 6; C. 4, X, *de iureiurando,* II, 24; C. 13, X, *de maioritate et obedientia,* I, 33.

closely the persons who were to make the profession.[144] Hence, those who assist, either with a deliberative or a consultative vote at a particular council, viz., the plenary council, are bound to make the profession of faith, according to the form approved by the Holy See.[145]

C. The Formula to be Used in the Profession of Faith

The obligation of making the profession of faith as imposed in canon 1406 can be fulfilled with the use of the present prescribed formula as printed in the Vatican edition of the Code, which is found preceding the text of the canons. This formula dates from the time of Pius IV, in 1564. The prerequisite of such an oath was substantially established and systematically organized in the legislation of the Council of Trent.[146] Aside from this formula, there is no special oath prescribed by ecclesiastical law. Thus the oath required by Pope X in the Motu Proprio, *Sacrorum Antistitum,* of September 1, 1910,[147] which would have been abolished in view of canon 6, n. 6,[148] had not the Holy Office previously declared that the Antimodernist Oath continues in force until the Holy See abrogates it expressly,[149] is not prescribed to the members of the plenary council.

The present formula of the profession of faith was first printed in the Constitution *"Iniunctum Nobis"* of Pope Pius IV, on No-

---

144 Conc. Trident., sess. XXIV, *de ref.*, cc. 1, 12.

145 Cf. canon 1406, § 1.

146 Conc. Trident., sess. XXIV, *de ref.*, cc. 1, 12; cf. Schroeder, *Canons and Decrees of the Council of Trent, Original Text with English Translations* (2. ed., Binghampton & New York: Vail-Ballou Press, Inc., 1950), pp. 190, 200-203 ff. (hereafter cited as *Canons and Decrees*).

147 *Fontes,* n. 689; *AAS,* II (1910), 635.

148 "Si qua ex ceteris disciplinaribus legibus, quae usque adhuc viguerunt, nec explicite nec implicite in Codice contineatur, ea vim omnem amisisse dicenda est, nisi in probatis liturgicis libris reperiatur, aut lex sit iuris divini sive positivi sive naturalis."

149 S. O., 22 martii 1918—*AAS,* X (1918), 136; *Fontes,* n. 689; Bouscaren, *Canon Law Digest* (3 vols. and Supplement through 1954, Milwaukee, Wisconsin: The Bruce Publishing Co., 1934-1954; 1955), I, 50 (hereafter cited as *Law Digest*).

vember 13, 1564.[150] Until now it has remained the same except for some small additions made by the Decree *Quod a priscis*.[151] The said formula is not to be confused with those professions of faith which are in use by reason of the provisions of liturgical laws, v. g., the formula of profession of faith taken by those who are about to be baptized,[152] the formula used by heretics when they return to the faith,[153] and the formula used at the ordination of priests.[154] These lie outside the field of the subject matter here traced and are governed by the existing liturgical laws, which have their own binding force.[155] For the facility of those who may have occasion to attend a plenary council as members, either with a deliberative or with a consultative vote, the above mentioned formula of the Profession of Faith will be found in the Appendix of this work.[156]

---

150 *Fontes,* n. 108.

151 S. C. C., 20 ian. 1877—*Fontes,* n. 4236.

152 Cf. *Rituale Romanum* (editio typica, Civitate Vaticana: Typis Polyglottis Vaticanis, 1952), tit. 2, c. 4, n. 32.

153 Cf. *Collectanea,* I, n. 1178.

154 Cf. *Pontificale Romanum,* "De Ordinatione Presbyteris."

155 Canon 2: ". . . Quare omnes liturgicae leges vim suam retinent, nisi earum aliqua in Codice expresse corrigatur." Cf. Aertnys-Damen, *Theologia Moralis* (2 vols., 11. ed., Taurinorum Augustae: Marietti, 1928), I, 218-219.

156 Page 118.

CHAPTER V

Object of Legislation

Article 1. Competence of the Council

A. Definition of the Code

The jurisdictional powers of the plenary council are derived through the law of the Code and are connected with the office which the prelates exercise in their own name when they are united in the conciliar assembly.[1] These powers must be classified, therefore, as ordinary ones,[2] and they include the legislative, executive and judicial powers throughout the whole territory under the jurisdiction of the council.[3] Today, the legislative function is the most dominant one among these powers.[4] The present law restricts greatly the judicial and the coative functions of the plenary council.[5]

The plenary council, in virtue of its legislative power, is competent to command and forbid, to encourage and dissuade. This power is not a mere sum of the powers of the individual bishops; it is a higher power conferred by law. It is above the episcopal power, since an individual bishop cannot legislate for anyone's territory except his own. The conciliar decrees have force in the territory for which the plenary council is being held. They are superior to the decrees of the individual bishops and local ordinaries who constitute the council. These decrees, therefore, surpass all episcopal and synodal laws.[6] All persons, inclusive of members

1 Cf. canon 290.

2 Cf. canon 197, § 1.

3 Wernz-Vidal, *Ius Canonicum*, II, 681; Beste, *Introductio*, p. 258.

4 Cf. canon 290.

5 Cf. canons 1557, §1; 2227, § 1.

6 Cf. Suarez, *De Legibus et Legislatore Deo*, Lib. VI, cap. 15, nn. 7, 8 (hereafter cited as *De Legibus*)—*Opera Omnia* (28 vols., ed. Vivès, Parisiis, 1856-1861), Vols. V, VI, *De Legibus et Legislatore Deo;* Chelodi, *Ius de Personis*, p. 372, nota 4; Benedictus XIV, *De Synodo*, Lib. XIV, cap. 5, n. 8; Wernz-Vidal, *Ius Canonicum*, II, 680.

of religious communities and without prejudice whatsoever to the exemptions granted to them by the Code,[7] are bound by the said decrees, provided these persons reside in the territory for which the legislation is made.[8] The territory thus affected includes all the dioceses and other localities the local ordinaries of which were invited to the council, even though the latter may not actually have attended it.[9] This jurisdiction of the plenary council, which has already been discussed,[10] is higher and even more extensive than that of the provincial council.[11]

B. Nature of the Competence.

Before the Code the competence of the plenary council depended upon the instruction of the Roman Pontiff. Hence, this competence was merely a delegated, and not an ordinary one. Under the Code the competence of the plenary council is one of ordinary powers, since it is based on the law itself.[12] In the plenary council the members discuss diligently and decide the matters that serve for the increase of faith, the guidance of morals, the correction of abuses, the settling of controversies and the uniformity of discipline.[13] Plenary councils, first of all, must subscribe to the solemnly and authentically defined truths of the Church. They are celebrated not to settle dogmatic controversies but to promote discipline.[14]

---

[7] Vermeersch-Creusen, *Epitome,* I, 315; Fagnanus, *Commentaria,* Lib. V, tit, 1, cap. 25, n. 87, p. 28.

[8] Cf. canons 13, 14, 92.

[9] Abbo-Hannan, *The Sacred Canons,* I, 332.

[10] Cf. *supra,* pp. 26-27.

[11] Toso, *Commentaria Minora,* III, 110.

[12] Wernz-Vidal, *Ius Canonicum,* II, 680; Coronata, *Institutiones,* I, 431; Cocchi, *Commentarium,* III, n. 127.

[13] Canon 290.—Patres in Concilio plenario vel provinciali congregati studiose inquirant as decernant quae ad fidei incrementum, ad moderandos mores, ad corrigendos abusus, ad controversias componendas, ad unam candemque disciplinam servandam vel inducendam, opportuna fore pro suo cuinsque territorio videantur. Cf. Ayrinhac, *Constitution of the Church,* p. 113.

[14] Chelodi, *Ius de Personis,* p. 372; Augustine, *A Commentary,* II, 305; Eichmann, *Lehrbuch des Kirchenrechts auf Grund des Codex Iuris Canonici* (6. ed., 3 vols., neu bearbeitet von Klaus Mösdorf, Paderborn: Schö-

Thus the members of the council must abstain from attempts to settle dogmatic controversies, though they are not prohibited from proposing, explaining and recommending the Catholic doctrines and the truths which are at least theologically certain, principally those which seem necessary and entirely related to renewing the increase of faith. The same thing is to be said regarding the preservation of morals. Questions which are still under discussion and consideration among the Doctors of the Church and are not yet exactly defined by the Holy See should be prudently avoided.[15]

To understand well the competence of the plenary council, it is essential to have a clear idea about the difference between a law *contra legem superiorem* and a law *praeter legem superiorem.* A law is contrary to a higher law when it tries to repeal what is commanded, or permits what is forbidden, or when it imposes an obligation repugnant to a higher law.[16] A law is *praeter legem superiorem* when it imposes an obligation which does not exist in virtue of a higher law. In spite of the fact that the distinction is clear in theory, nevertheless it is difficult at times to know in practice if there really exists an actual opposition between a higher and a lower law.[17] It follows that the legislative power of the plenary council does not allow the enacting of laws contrary to the general law of the Church. The members of this council cannot

---

ningh, 1949-1950), I, 359; Coronata, *loc cit.;* Wernz, *Ius Decretalium,* I, n. 181.

[15] Benedictus XIV, *De Synodo,* Lib. VII, cap. 1, nn. 1 ff.; Lib. XIII, cap. 3, nn. 1-2; Fagnanus, *Commentaria,* Lib. V, tit. 1, cap. 25, n. 62, p. 27; Abbo-Hannan, *The Sacred Canons,* I, 331.

[16] Suarez, *De Legibus,* Lib. VI, c. 27, n. 2.

[17] This point may be illustrated with an interesting example found in the *Acta Apostolicae Sedis,* Vol. XIII (1921), 228-230: A certain council which had been held before the Code came into force forbade the sending of Mass stipends outside one's diocese without the permission of the local ordinary. There was disagreement as to whether this prohibition was *contra Codicem* or *praeter Codicem.* The Congregation of the Council was asked to reply to the question: "An et quomodo dispositio Concilii provincialis sustineatur in casu?" The reply was: "Quoad missas fundatas, vel ad instar manualium, vel manuales datas intuitu causae piae: Affirmative; in reliquis servetur can. 838 Codicis Iuris Canonici." Cf. Bouscarem, *Law Digest,* I, 399, 400.

prohibit what is expressly and clearly permitted by the general law, unless the general law itself gives them this power.[18]

To invade the jurisdiction of a legislative superior and to countermand his decrees is both unlawful and invalid. Any warranted power to do so would sap the whole structure of the hierarchy of the Church. A right of contradicting the laws of a superior would suggest that the power of the superior relies upon the inferior, which is at all costs inadmissible.[19] The Fathers of the council must be on their guard lest they enact a decree which might run contrary to a higher law. An indult should be asked when a certain decree of that type is desired. It can be said, therefore, that the celebration of a plenary council is propitious for asking favors. Such favors when granted can be published appropriately as an appendix to the legislation.

Whenever a *dubium iuris* exists, that is, when it is doubtful whether a permission is positively conceded by law in a certain case, or whether it is a point upon which the law remains silent, the legislative inferior is not restricted, for a doubtful law does not bind him.[20] Decrees which are opposed to any of the privileges and exemptions granted either by the Holy Father or by common law to the members of religious communities are certainly invalid, but it should be remembered that the council can legislate in those matters in which the members of religious communities are subject to the local ordinaries.[21]

C. *Decisions of the Council*

In the plenary council all important decisions and points of procedure, like the order of business, the opening and the adjournment of the council, its transfer or prolongation, are determined by the presiding officer.[22] The office of presiding at the council is

---

18 Wernz, *Ius Decretalium,* II, n. 756; Abbo-Hannan, *The Sacred Canons,* I, 331.

19 Suarez, *De Legibus,* Lib. VI, cap. 36, n. 4.

20 Canon 15: Leges, etiam irritantes et rehabilitantes, in dubio iuris non urgent . . .

21 Benedictus XIV, *De Synodo,* Lib. IX, cap. 15, nn. 1, 4.

22 Canon 288.—In Concilio sive plenario sive provinciali praeses, habito, si de provinciali agatur, Patrum consensu, determinat ordinem servandum

conferred by law,[23] and does not depend upon the consent of the members of the council, for the Apostolic Legate acts in the name of the Holy Father.[24] With the exception of the right of convoking the council and of presiding at its sessions, the Apostolic Legate and all those who have a deliberative vote share equally in the conciliar decisions and decrees. The consent of the prelates gathered together is requisite for determining the conciliar decrees. An absolute majority vote is always required; a relative majority vote is not sufficient.[25] Although the requirement of a majority vote is not stated explicitly in the Code, such a requirement has always been the accepted practice of plenary councils.[26]

The Church, aware of the advantages of united action, stresses the value of discussion as a factor in the working of plenary councils. The Code itself indicates that a discreet consultation is necessary for a sound administration, and obliges all residential bishops to seek capitular consent in nineteen cases,[27] and advice in twenty-nine.[28] The seeking of consent or counsel is not just a mere formality; to act without seeking the required consent is to act invalidly. To reject the advice of the majority without a proportionate reason is to violate the clear provision of the Code.[29] Even the popes hear the opinions of others so as to become conversant with the arguments for each side before taking action. Thus the

---

in quaestionibus examinandis et ipsum Concilium aperit, transfert, prorogat, absolvit.

[23] Cf. canon 281.

[24] Cf. *supra*, p. 32.

[25] Suarez, *De Legibus*, Lib. VI, cap. 15, n. 6: " . . . talis est jurisdictio Concilii ut actus ejus communi consensu seu majoris partis fieri debeant . . . "; Cance-Arquer, *El Código*, I, n. 287.

[26] I Council of Nicaea (325), can. 5—Bruns, I, 15; II Council of Arles (443/452), can. 5—Bruns, II, 131; c. 7, X, *de temporibus ordinationum et qualitate ordinandorum*, I, 11; IV Council of Toledo (633), can. 4—Bruns, I, 222; *Glossa ordinaria* ad c. 1, C. XV, q. 7, s. v. *concilii;* Fagnanus, *Commentaria*, Lib. V, tit. 1; cap. 25, n. 34; Ceillier, *Histoire Générale*, II, 432.

[27] Cf. Trombetta, *De Consensu et Consilio Capituli Cathedralis iuxta Codicem Iuris Canonici* (Neapoli, 1926), pp. 17-19 (hereafter cited as *De Consensu*).

[28] Cf. Trombetta, *De Consensu*, pp. 20-22.

[29] Cf. canon 105.

laws enacted in the plenary council are the result of consultation and discussion which are held *collegialiter*. The Papal Legate as a member has one vote, but if the divergent votes on any point are equal he can determine the issue by casting an added vote[30] which is called a decisive vote, for he is not merely a *"primus inter pares."*[31]

Article 2. General Object of Legislation Mentioned in the Code

Canon 290.—Patres in Concilio plenario vel provinciali congregati studiose inquirant ac decernant quae ad fidei incrementum, ad moderandos mores, ad corrigendos abusus, ad controversias componendas, ad unam eandemque disciplinam servandam vel inducendam, opportuna fore pro suo cuiusque territorio videantur.

Plenary councils legitimately convoked, held and approved or recognized by the Holy See, are the legislators for the territories from which the assembled bishops come. Such legislative power given by the Roman Pontiff to such a council as a college is exercised licitly and validly, though it should not be considered as an arithmetical sum of the rights of the various bishops. The jurisdiction, therefore, of the plenary council is a superior authority to which each and every bishop is subject.[32]

The above cited canon states in rough outline and determines in general terms what is to be submitted to the deliberation and consultation of the Fathers. It resembles principally the laws of the IV general Council of the Lateran (1215) and of the Council of Trent (1545-1563).[33] It is not an absolutely all-inclusive list or

[30] Cf. canon 101, § 1; Coronata, *Institutiones,* I, 432; Chelodi, *Ius de Personis,* p. 374.

[31] Cf. *supra*, p. 32.

[32] A decision of the Holy See given on September 10, 1896, will serve to illustrate this point: Q. I.—"Utrum Episcopi in concilio sive plenario sive provinciali legitime coadunati vera potestate legislativa potiri censeantur? Q. II.—Utrum decreta Conciliorum sive plenariorum sive provincialium a S. Sede in forma communi sive specifica confirmata vel approbata vel saltem recognita, omnimode vi careant, nisi in statuta diocesana iam fuerit incorporata?" Respondit: "Ad I.—Affirmative. Ad. II.—Negative. Et ad mentem."—*Fontes,* n. 1184; *Collectanea,* II, n. 1952.

[33] Cf. Conc. Trident., sess. XXIV, *de ref.,* c. 2: "Provincialia concilia

enumeration of the purposes of conciliar decrees, but rather a demonstrative one.[34] In any event, the Fathers of the Council must search out zealously (*studiose inquirant*) the matters that call for legislation.

A. Increase of Faith

The Catholic Church has always claimed to have been assigned by Our Lord Jesus Christ as the only guardian and authorized teacher and interpreter of His truths. This well-known fact is proved by history. This authority of teaching the word of God belongs to the Church in virtue of its very institution. The way of exercising this office is a part of its power of jurisdiction as contrasted with the powers of orders.[35] This right and duty, independent of any civil power, is exercized by the Church in many different ways, and one among these is through the plenary councils. Thus the bishops, though they do not either individually or when assembled in a particular council possess infallibility in their teaching, yet are truly doctors and teachers of the faithful commited to their care under the authority of the Roman Pontiff.[36]

To promote the increase of faith is the task committed to the plenary council, but not the power of defining matters of faith, for infallibility is not the attribute of a plenary council. By its nature, the supreme infallible authority in the Church is the only

---

sicubi omissa sunt, pro moderandis moribus, corrigendis excessibus, controversiis componendis, aliisque ex sacris canonibus permissis renoventur." Cf. also the IV general Council of the Lateran, can. 6: " . . . metropolitani singulis annis cum suis suffraganeis provincialia ne omittant concilia celebrare, in quibus de corrigendis excessibus et moribus reformandis, praesertim in clero, diligentem habeant cum Dei timore tractatum, canonicas regulas, et maxime quae statutae sunt in hoc generali concilio, relegentes, ut eas faciant observari, debitam poenam transgressoribus infligendo."—Mansi, XXII, 991; c. 25, X, *de accusationibus, inquisitionibus et denuntiationibus,* V, 1.

[34] Murphy, *Legislative Powers,* p. 53.

[35] Wernz-Vidal, *Ius Canonicum,* IV, Pars II, 3.

[36] Canon 1326.—Episcopi quoque, licet singuli vel etiam in Conciliis particularibus congregati infallibilitate docendi non polleant, fidelium tamen suis curis commissorum, sub auctoritate Romani Pontificis, veri doctores seu magistri sunt.

one empowered to act on matters of faith which are difficult and controverted.[37] The plenary council, however, may denounce heresies, alert the faithful regarding wrong tendencies, and warn the faithful against them. Thus the obligation of protecting the Church against its enemies by exposing misrepresentations, by proclaiming true Catholic doctrine, and by instituting means to publish it among the people rests on the assembled prelates who are constituted as true teachers.[38]

The laws by which the members of the Church are externally assisted in the profession of their faith are called disciplinary.[39] The already authentically defined or theologically certain teachings of the Church are the bases of these laws. For a more spiritual formation of the faithful and an increase of their faith, disciplinary regulations of the clergy are also needed.

B. Preservation of Morals

Not only matters of faith but also matters of morals are in their definition reserved to the infallible authority of the Church.[40] Thus a plenary council can deal with these matters only regarding their discipline, that is, the directive how to live in a Christian manner, as founded on good morals. Dangers to morals must be assiduously explained. Whatever is necessary to promote the spiritual welfare of the people in the respective territory must be commanded and decreed. Among matters dealt with in the council, regulations of this kind should be given a prominent position.[41] For their far-reaching effects on the moral and religious life of the laity, in general, legislation concerning vocations to the priesthood and to the religious state should not be overlooked.[42] For the United States

[37] Canon 1323. Cf. Augustine, *A Commentary*, II, 305; Wernz, *Ius Decretalium*, I, n. 181; Chelodi, *Ius de Personis*, p. 372; Fagnanus, *Commentaria*, Lib. V, tit. 1, cap. 25, n. 82.

[38] De Meester, *Compendium*, II, 115.

[39] Vermeersch-Creusen, *Epitome*, I, 16.

[40] Cf. canon 1323; Augustine, *A Commentary*, II, 305.

[41] Conc. Trident., sess. XXIV, *de ref.*, c. 2; Fagnanus, *Commentaria*, Lib. V, tit. 1, cap. 25, n. 13.

[42] Canon 1354 of the Code states that each diocese should have its own seminary, wherever it is possible, and larger dioceses should establish a major and a minor seminary as well.

of America, the legislation of the II Plenary Council of Baltimore required that in each ecclesiastical province there should be at least one major and one minor seminary.[43]

C. Correction of Abuses

If anyone's conduct causes scandal or occasions a serious disturbance for the public order, there is ground for a correction or a rebuke. Abuses, therefore, whether they are violations of the disciplinary law of the Church or of the divine law, must be met with determination by the conciliar assembly according to the prudent discretion of its lawful members. These Fathers must, nevertheless, bear in mind that they are shepherds and not oppressors, and that they ought so to provide over those subject to them as not to lord it over them,[44] but to love them as children and brethren. They must strive by exhortation and admonition to deter their subjects from what is unlawful, so that they will not need by means of punishment to coerce them as transgressors. Regarding those who should happen to sin because of human weakness, the Apostle's command should be observed, namely that they be entreated, reproved, and rebuked in all kindness and patience,[45] since benevolence toward those who are to be corrected often effects more than severity, exhortation more than threat, and charity more than force.[46] If, however, on account of the gravity of the offense a serious moral abuse should arise, in such a case a command with perhaps a penal sanction is needed, in order that discipline, which is so salutary and necessary for the people, may be preserved. The Fathers of the plenary council, therefore, must join hands and take united measures to stem and remove all kinds of abuses.

D. Settlement of Controversies

By the phrase *"ad controversias componendas"*[47] is not meant a dogmatic or theological settlement. This phrase concerns ques-

[43] *Conc. Plen. Baltim. II, Acta et Decreta,* nn. 172-174; *Coll. Lac.,* III, 449-450.

[44] Cf. I Pet., 5: 2 ff.; Cc. 1-9, D. XLV; canon 2214, § 2.

[45] Cf. II Tim., 4: 2.

[46] C. 6, D. XLV.

[47] Cf. canon 290.

tions of discipline, such as the education of the clergy and the faithful in seminaries and schools, the administration of the sacraments, and the defining of boundaries for parishes.[48] Controversies which have become dangerous to the interests of religion the Fathers of the council must settle by commanding silence or by explaining the already defined doctrine of the Church. This power of the plenary council, though it is scarcely practical today, yet is still in existence and has never been revoked.[49]

E. Uniformity of Discipline

Uniformity, as it has already been pointed out,[50] is greatly desired by the Holy See. It is obviously clear that the utility of uniformity is not without limits, for the more extensive is the territory that is involved, the greater is the room for a discrepancy of practice, and hence the greater is the desirability of allowing a reasonable freedom for a divergency in practice.

Under modern circumstances uniformity of discipline is of particular utility and corresponds to the aims of the current law.[51] This is practically true nowadays when, through the easy and rapid ways of transportation, and the constant flow of inter-city and inter-state business and social activities, the relationship between dioceses is made closer than heretofore. In order then to avoid a wide discrepancy of discipline, which could weaken the efficient administration of each diocese, and to avoid variations in the observance of ecclesiastical laws,[52] which could readily become an occasion of bewilderment to the faithful, there should be a uniformity of discipline. Otherwise, scandal, carelessness, and a lessened fidelity to the laws of the Church could follow almost necessarily.[53]

It is sometimes a difficult task for a bishop alone to settle the various problems of discipline encountered in his diocese. With the help of other bishops and local ordinaries of different dioceses

---

[48] Augustine, *A Commentary,* II, 305.

[49] De Meester, *Compendium,* II, 116.

[50] Cf. *supra,* chapter IV, art. 1.

[51] Chelodi, *Ius de Personis,* p. 372, note 4.

[52] E. g., laws of fasting and abstinence.

[53] Guilday, *The Life and Times of John England* (2 vols., New York: The America Press, 1927), II, 108.

and provinces, who are united in action in a plenary council, and after serious and mutual deliberations and suggestions, the local bishop finds his task much easier. In this way also the government of every diocese will be strengthened or perhaps even effectively reformed.

Article 3. Particular Object of Legislation

Canon 290 determines in general terms the subject matter of the plenary council. No particular points whatsoever are reserved by the Code to the plenary council as they are reserved in the case of provincial councils and diocesan synods.[54] Whenever the Holy See grants permission for the holding of a plenary council, it is assumed that the bishops are conversant with the needs of their clergy and people. The minutes of their regular meetings should provide them with matters which may opportunely be considered. The bishops have to fix their attention to the subject matter which is proposed for discussion. The Code, indeed, does not prescribe such preliminary preparations, but in practice it is always desirable and, indeed, necessary. Thus, in diocesan synods the Code permits preliminary meetings, and orders that a scheme of the agenda be supplied in advance.[55] Such procedure by analogy establishes a good argument for its practice in any plenary council. The seeking of consent or counsel is not just a mere formality, because to act without the required consent is to act invalidly, as to reject the advice of the majority without a proportionate reason is to violate the clear provision of the law.[56]

To introduce extensive legislation is undesirable. Excessive severity and innovation in the legislation should be avoided,[57] for it is a dictate of common sense that excessive legislation defeats its own purpose. The authority of the individual bishops should not be unduly restricted, and a suitable margin must be left for provincial legislation. If possible, the legislative enactments must

[54] Cf. canons 1507; 1909, § 1; 472, 2°; 895.

[55] Cf. canon 360.

[56] Cf. canon 105.

[57] Chelodi, *Ius de Personis*, p. 372, note 4.

be generally few and mild, because benevolence often counts for more than power.[58]

As a model for particular legislation the order of the Code is ideal, since the sequence in legislative matters is indeed excellent.[59] Certain canons are really of outstanding practical significance and they could well be reproduced, but the choice must be always made judiciously. Matters which do not appear in the Code, but are important points for legislation, should be submitted to the Fathers for discussion in the plenary sessions.

A. Conferring of Parishes by Concursus

When provision is made for the care of souls, the most suitable priests should always be selected, since the eternal salvation of numerous souls is always concerned. Many souls may be saved or lost in consequence of the fruitful or barren ministry of a priest. The degree of fitness required in an appointee is oftentimes difficult to determine. Hence it would not be without profit for the Fathers of a plenary council to enact particular legislation, with reference to the conferring of a parish upon a previous *concursus*, in the matter of gaining the needed appraisal regarding a candidate's learning as a condition of fitness for his appointment.

In the fourth paragraph of canon 459[60] two kinds of *concursus* are mentioned: one is special, as described by Benedict XIV, and the other is general, which differs from the special. The general *concursus* is an examination held at stated times, the results of which are utilized in the filling of future vacancies, while the special *concursus* is the competitive examination in the form prescribed by law which is held when a parish falls vacant.

The III Plenary Council of Baltimore (1884),[61] in reference to the appointment of irremovable rectors for parochial churches

---

[58] Cf. canon 2214, § 2.

[59] Cf. Berutti, *Institutiones Iuris Canonici* (6 vols., Vol. II, Pars II, et Vol. V adhuc sub praelio, Taurini-Romae: Marietti, 1936-43), I, nn. 32-34 (hereafter cited as *Institutiones*).

[60] "In regionibus in quibus paroeciarum provisio fit per concursum specialem ad normam const. Benedicti XIV *Cum illud,* 14 Dec. 1742, sive generalem, haec forma retineatur, donec Sedes Apostolica aliud decreverit."

[61] Chapter V, *De Rectoribus Inamovibilibus,* n. 26.

decreed: (a) that a priest must have exercized the sacred ministry in the diocese for at least ten years; (b) that during these years he must have proved himself capable of administering a parish, and (c) that he must take part in the *concursus* according to the form set down in the constitution *Cum illud* of Pope Benedict XIV. Nevertheless, at the request of the Hierarchy of America, the Sacred Congregation of the Council abolished this law of the last Plenary Council of Baltimore, and decreed that from then on the appointment of pastors, whether irremovable or removable, was to be made according to the provision of canon 459, § 3.[62] Thus, practically, this matter no longer holds good for the United States of America, but in other countries where a use of the *concursus* still obtains, the Fathers of the plenary council can establish legislation regarding it.

1. Desire of the Council of Trent

The general way of appointing a pastor to a benefice upon a previous *concursus* is given in detail by the Council of Trent.[63] The main aim of the *concursus* was to detect the best man for the vacant office or benefice and to bar the unfit from receiving an office or benefice which could not be filled properly by them. The said Council also stated that for all vacant parishes examinations were likewise to be held.

Although the conditions, the subject-matter, and the method of this competitive examination were perfected by Pope Pius V,[64] Clement XI,[65] and Benedict XIV,[66] the wording of the decree of the Council of Trent was in itself somewhat vague. It seemed wise to clarify several points of the full text, so that confusion in its

---

[62] Letter of the Apostolic Delegate, Aug. 1, 1933—*Homiletic and Pastoral Review,* XXXII (1931), 189-190.

[63] Cf. sess. XXIV, *de ref.*, c. 18.

[64] Const. *In conferendis,* 18 mart. 1567—*Fontes,* n. 119; const. *Apostolatus Officium,* 19 aug. 1567—*Bullarum Diplomatum et Privilegiorum Sanctorum Romanorum Pontificum Taurinensis Editio* (24 vols. in 25, 1857-1883), VII, 555-605 (hereafter cited as *Bull. Rom.*).

[65] Litt. encycl. *Quo parochiales,* 10 jan. 1721—*Acta Sanctae Sedis* (41 vols., Romae, 1865-1908), VII (1872), 367 sqq. (hereafter cited as *ASS*).

[66] Const. *Cum illud,* 14 dec. 1742—*ASS,* VII (1872), 371 sqq.

application would be avoided. For this purpose certain specific rules were laid down by the above-mentioned popes in their constitutions and encyclicals. In the absence of any change of law in the present or for the future, these same rules should be followed: 1—The bishop, when he receives notice of the vacancy of a parish, should immediately appoint a suitable administrator, who will fill the parochial office during the interregnum. 2—Public notice should be given of a *concursus* to be held, and a suitable time set during which the names, information, and documents of the competitors should be given to the chancellor. 3—The examination should deal not only with the knowledge of each candidate, but also with his age, his morals, his past services, his ability, and the qualities which may fit him for the vacant office. 4—After the examination, the synodal examiners are to give their findings and vote to the bishop, who himself is to select the candidate. 5—If any candidate appeals from the *concursus* because of the examiners' or the bishop's suspected judgment the whole proceedings are to be repeated before the judge of appeal.

During the vacancy of a see the administator or, if the see is impeded, the vicar general sends out the notice of the *concursus.* All the priests of the diocese and even those outside the diocese who were engaged in parish work, unless their own respective ordinaries prohibit them from doing so, could take part in the *concursus,* although naturally a diocesan priest had preference over an outsider.

2. Means of Expediting the *Concursus*

It would really prove problematical to enter the *concursus* if there were no norms at all for properly conducting and expediting the *concursus.* Thus, the same questions must be given to those who will take part in it.[67] The questions must be answered and the case must be solved by everybody during the same interval of time, and the homily must be written by the candidates within the same allotted duration of time. Everyone must have the same equal allowance of time. The examination is to be in writing, and

[67] Viz., the same case in moral theology, and the same text of the Gospel on which to write a homily.

all competitors must be assigned to the same room. During the examinations no outsider shall be admitted nor shall anyone leave the examination room until the papers are handed in. For uniformity's sake, the answers are to be made in Latin, but the homily is to be written in the vernacular. It would be preferable that all the answers be made in handwriting. The chancellor, the examiners, and the bishop or his vicar shall countersign the papers after they are handed in.[68]

On the assumption that redress is sought, this must be interposed within ten days after the examinations.[69] Every appeal that comes from any suffragan see goes to the metropolitan, and any appeal from the metropolitan goes to the designated see or bishop previously established by law, or it could be made to the Holy See, according as the circumstances might suggest. All appeals are *in devolutivo,* and no new document can be introduced in the appeal.[70]

B. Disabled and Aged Priests

1. Their Support

"Let the priests that rule well, be esteemed worthy of double honor, especially they who labour in word and doctrine."[71] These words were the admonition of St. Paul to his disciple Timothy, who at that period had in hand the entire appointment and distribution of the means contributed for the purposes of religion. Nothing can be more just than that the provision for the clergy should be the principal object of its application.[72]

As always, the Church is very solicitous for an adequate care of its clergy in their old age and disability. Even in China, where the Church is in straitened circumstances, provision is made for the support of retired priests.[73] The priest's income must be sufficient

---

[68] Const. *Cum illud,* 14 dec. 1742, § 7, 1-7—C.I.C., Docum. IV.

[69] Pius V, const. *In conferendis,* 18 mart. 1567—*Fontes,* n. 119.

[70] Benedictus XIV, const. *Cum illud,* 14 dec. 1742, § 15—C.I.C., Docum. IV.

[71] I Tim., 5:17.

[72] Cf. II Tim., 2:6:—"The husbandman that laboreth must first partake of the fruits."

[73] *Praxis Missionalis in Vicariatu Apostolico de Inchang* (Wuchung: The Franciscan Press, 1935), p. 52, n. 92. Regarding the removal of clerics

to enable him to have enough saved for his support when the time of retirement comes either because of old age or in view of disability, unless he is assured of a pension when he retires.

Priests, therefore, if ordained on the title of a benefice, when worn out by labor or old age, or when incapacitated by sickness or by accident, will come to enjoy the income of a benefice, which income will be large enough to afford them a suitable pension when they retire, besides adequately supporting the new incumbent in the benefices.[74]

2. Contributions to Their Support

Unfortunately this system of providing pensions for retired priests as outlined in canon 1429, § 2, does not become applicable for a majority of the priests in many parts of the world,[75] since most of these priests are not ordained to major orders on the title of a benefice, by which they would be supported during their active ministry and from which they would draw a pension when they retired, but on the title of service of the diocese. The title of service of the diocese, as a matter of fact, was approved because there were not sufficient benfices for the support of the priests who were needed for the care of souls in a diocese. Besides, a priest ordained on the title of service of the diocese is seldom assigned for the rest of his active ministry to a certain parish. Generally taken, a secular priest, in the course of his ministry, serves successively several parishes.

---

from a benefice because of an incurable disease and without provision for sufficient support, Reiffenstuel said: " . . . si enim clerici aegrotantes tam inhumaniter tractarentur, ceteri detererentur in clericatu."—*Jus Canonicum Universum* (5 vols. in 7, Parisiis, 1864-1870; Vol. IV, 1867), Vol. IV, Lib. III, tit. 6, n. 3, p. 1.

[74] Cf. canon 1429, § 2.

[75] On canon 1429, § 2, Coronata comments strongly: "De iure ferendo, si semel nostrum votum exprimere licet, optandum est ut Ordinariis maior circa hoc libertas relinquatur. Sunt etiam apud nos paroeciae pinguissimae quarum reditibus subveniri posset facile vicariis cooperatoribus, qui saepe saepius in magna vereantur paupertate, cum non spernenda populi christiani admiratione. Utinam concedatur Ordinariis locorum modus his incommodis subveniendi, concedendo ipsis ius pensiones imponendi etiam beneficiis paroecialibus."—*Institutiones*, II, 391.

Instances have occurred wherein meritorious priests, after a faithful discharge of their duty, were neglected and left in great destitution. Justice demands that this should not be so. There are even cases in which the clergyman has need of the aid he deserves, but lacks a sufficient claim upon any special church that would entitle him to require that it should support him. The Code, unfortunately, has not provided a practical system of securing support for disabled and aged priests ordained on the title of service of the diocese. Accordingly the Fathers of a plenary council should for this purpose devise a system which will in no manner be contrary to the enactments in the Code.

A mutual assistance society among the clergy, to be formed and directed by the local ordinary, as specified in the last paragraph of Decree 71 of the III Plenary Council of Baltimore, may provide the preferable method of supplying support for such priests.[76]

3. Other Means of Support

One of the reasons why some of the diocesan clergy enter the religious orders is the constant sense of insecurity to sickness and old age. Priests, we all know, are prohibited by the canons of the Church[77] from being engaged in business, so that they may be wholly occupied in their ministerial duties.[78] The emoluments they receive are moderate, and sometimes even wretchedly small. They are also faced with supplications from the distressed, and with demands for the general purposes of religion, which suffice to

---

[76] "Modus alius praedictae necessitati prospiciendi in eo est, ut societas mutui subsidii inter presbyteros constituatur quae societas aerarii seu pecuniae congestae administrationem, item Episcopo praeside, curabit. Huic societati unusquisque sacerdos dioecesi adscriptus nomen dare urgeatur."—*Acta et Decreta Concilii Plenarii Baltimorensis III*, n. 71. This enactment of the Council of Baltimore has not been abrogated by the Code; it belongs to the class of particular legislation *praeter Codicem*. Cf. Barrett, *A Comparative Study of the Councils of Baltimore and the Code of Canon Law*, (The Catholic University of America, 1932), Chapter III, tit. 4; "Conciliar Laws abrogated and Not Abrogated by the Code," *The Jurist*, II (1942), 63.

[77] Cf. canons 142 and 2380.

[78] II Tim., 2:3,4: "No man, being a soldier to God, entangleth himself with secular businesses; that he may please him to whom he hath engaged himself."

deprive them of the means to lay up for themselves provisions for old age or infirmity. Some only have a hand-to-mouth sort of existence, and, hence, no chance to provide for the future.

In such contingencies, if a fitting support for disabled or aged priests cannot be secured either by the arranging of a pension according to the provisions of canon 1429, § 2, or by the establishing of a clerical mutual benefit society, as mentioned above, then the Fathers of a plenary council, aware of this situation, should remedy it by warning the faithful of their duty to support their priests, and legislate that a collection for the support of retired priests be taken up in all parishes. The Code does not forbid that an annual collection of voluntary offerings be sollicited for the support of the clergy; it only prohibits that a constantly recurring tax be imposed.[79] It is only natural that priests who are no longer able to carry on their ministry be furnished in their needs by those whom they have served, lest they who are already suffering be further afflicted.

The generosity of the faithful, spurred by their appreciation of the services rendered by their priests, will certainly guarantee the success of a collection solicited for the support of the retired priests. "What do they do for priests who retire because of old age or for being disabled?" This is the common question one often hears from the devout laity on the lack of a suitable retreat for aged and disabled priests. An annual collection may well furnish a fitting and ample support for the disabled and aged priests. The fund which would be established through the receipts from this annual collection could be further enhanced by the charitable bequests, so that eventually a sufficient capital would emerge for this charitable purpose.

In case the proper support of these priests cannot be left to the uncertain results of the collection, then the Fathers of the council should apply for an indult which would permit the local ordinaries to levy a tax on the parishes of their territory in order to insure enough funds for the proper support of the aged and disabled priests. There is no doubt that the solicitude of the Holy See for

[79] Canon 1505.

the disabled and aged priests would guarantee a sympathetic hearing for the plea seeking this indult.

As a good guide for the Fathers of a plenary council in making legislation for the support of the aged and disabled priests, the following summary is submitted: 1) The ordinary may establish suitable pensions for retiring pastors or assistant pastors for the income of the benefice from which they retire;[80] 2) in case the prescription of canon 1429, § 2, cannot be carried out, the ordinary should establish a mutual assistance society;[81] 3) in case of the impracticability of the two preceding methods a collection for the support of the disabled and aged priests may be instituted in the parishes of the diocese, and finally 4) there may be requested a special indult to allow the local ordinaries to levy a moderate tax on the parishes to establish a fund for the support of the disabled and aged priests.

C. *Suspended Priests*

The local ordinaries, as shepherds of their flock, have the native and proper right of inflicting punishments on refractory priests.[82] This right is native and proper because it belongs to the Church, and thus to the local ordinaries, not through a concession made by human power or through a gradual evolution of history or as the accidental result of circumtances, but through the legitimate endowment conferred on it by Christ, who founded the Church as a perfected and autonomous society entitled to such a right.[83]

Of all the penalties which the Church has instituted for the disciplining of its priests, the one most employed is suspension. This right of the Church to suspend its priests follows as a consequence from the Church's status as a perfectly autonomous society. The Church has, it is true, a supreme legislative and judiciary power, but its mission to save souls would be wholly fruitless, if it did not at the same time have the right to coerce the contumacious[84]

---

[80] Canon 1429, § 2.

[81] *Acta et Decreta Concilii Plenarii Baltimorensis III*, n. 71.

[82] Cf. canon 2376; Conc. Trident., sess. VI, *de ref.*, c. 3.

[83] Abbo-Hannan, *The Sacred Canons*, II, 797.

[84] Canon 2213; Ottaviani, *Institutiones Iuris Publici Ecclesiastici* (2.

by means of the infliction of spiritual or also of temporal penalties.[85] It is important that in every well constituted society there should be an authority to exclude the unworthy, to remove corrupt magistrates from office, or at least to suspend temporarily the exercise of their powers.[86]

1. House of Penance

Since the spiritual and temporal progress of the Church as a society would be impaired and the attainment of its end would be rendered difficult by scandalous lives among its officials, the Church is certainly within the scope of its power in instituting a penalty that affects its officials exclusively. This penalty is what we know today as suspension. This penalty, whether medicinal or vindictive, may prohibit a cleric from exercising the rights of his office, his power of orders, or the administration of any benefice he might possess.[87] For the correction of the suspended priest or the reparation of the scandal, the ordinary could according to his conscientious judgment, command or forbid in serious cases the suspended priest to stay in some certain place, or consign him in a house of penance.[88] There are many episcopal sees wherein a house of this kind is wanting. Is it because there are no suspended priests in such dioceses? Even granted that this be true, one may note that a house of penance is not merely a house of correction; it could serve also as a retreat house for the clergy when there is no suspended priest staying in it. Thus, it would be recommendable to the Fathers of a plenary council to enact legislation for the erection of houses of penance wherever needed in the territories for which the council is being held.

Every ordinary should be temperate in the determination of the time a suspended priest should stay in a house of penance. Since the jurisdiction of each local ordinary is confined within or re-

---

ed., 2 vols., Typis Polyglottis Vaticanis, 1935-1936), I, 324 (hereafter cited as *Institutiones*).

[85] Ottaviani, *op. cit.*, I, 323.

[86] Wernz, *Ius Decretalium,* VI, n. 147.

[87] Canons 2278, § 1; 2298, n. 2.

[88] Canon 2302.

stricted to the boundaries of his see, he may not order a suspended priest to leave his diocese and to stay in a certain place in the territory of another local ordinary, unless the latter consents or has given a general consent by allowing the establishment of a house of penance with the understanding that the ordinaries of the surrounding dioceses will be permitted to send their priests there for the purpose of doing penance and amending their lives.[89]

2. Their Support

The Code provides that every secular cleric who has received major orders is entitled to support unless he has been guilty of crime in consequence of which he had suffered deposition, perpetual deprivation of the clerical garb, or degradation.[90] If a deposed cleric suffer real need, the ordinary in his charity should try to afford him what would suffice for his livelihood, lest he be driven to mendicancy to the discredit of the clerical state.[91] The cleric, however, has no claim in justice to this support.

A cleric cannot expect support from the Church while contumaciously persevering in a sin to which is attached a censure, and with much more reason the ordinary has no duty to provide support for a cleric who has incurred a censure which, either after sentence has been pronounced or by the very commission of the crime, involves the loss of income, for in any of these cases the cleric can, upon true repentance, secure absolution from his sin as well as from the censure attached to it.[92] Suspension is accordingly considered here not as a censure but as a vindictive penalty,

---

[89] Cf. canon 2301; Coronata, *Institutiones,* IV, 272; Wernz-Vidal, *Ius Canonicum,* VII, 388; Vermeersch-Creusen, *Epitome,* III, 301.

[90] Canons 980, § 1; 2298, 6°; 2299, § 3; 2304; 2305; Smith, *Elements of Ecclesiastical Law* (3 vols., Vol. III, New York, 1888), III, 95 (hereafter cited as *Elements*); Sipos, *Enchiridion Iuris Canonici* (3 ed., Pecs: Ex Typographia "Haladas R. T.," 1936), p. 947 (hereafter cited as *Enchiridion*); Findlay, *Canonical Norms Governing the Deposition and Degradation of Clerics,* The Catholic University of America Canon Law Studies, n. 130 (Washington, D.C.: The Catholic University of America Press, 1941), pp. 167 ff. (hereafter cited as *Deposition and Degradation*).

[91] Canon 2303, § 2.

[92] Cf. canons 2241; 2255, § 1; 2266; 2286.

for the latter alone will deprive him of part or of all of his income.[93]

The principal vindictive penalties which affect the income of clerics upon whom they are imposed are: temporary or perpetual suspension either *ab officio* or *a divinis*,[94] deprivation of one's benefice or office,[95] or deprivation of some right connected with an office or benefice,[96] deposition[97] perpetual deprivation of the clerical garb[98] and degradation.[99] These penalties may be imposed for a temporary or a perpetual duration, or for an unspecified duration of time, or *ad nutum superioris.*[100]

It has been the constant teaching of the Church that a priest, for the honor of his sacred character, should not be forced to beg or to work at an unbecoming trade.[101] One of the reasons why a priest who has become suspended through the imposition of a vindictive penalty has a right to be supported by the ordinary is that he still belongs to the ranks of the clergy, albeit he is judged not worthy of performing the duties of an office. It is the dignity of his priestly state which demands that he be supported.[102]

---

[93] Canons 2286; 2291, 12°; Vermeersch-Creusen, *Epitome,* III, 294.

[94] Canon 2298, 2°.

[95] Canon 2298, 6°.

[96] Canon 2298, 4°.

[97] Canon 2303; Wernz-Vidal, *Ius Canonicum,* VII, 396; Coronata, *Institutiones,* IV, 274; Beste, *Introductio,* p. 952.

[98] Canon 2304; Wernz-Vidal, *op. cit.,* VII, 399; Vermeersch-Creusen, *Epitome,* III, 304.

[99] Canon 2305; Wernz-Vidal, *op. cit.,* VII, 406; Coronata, *op. cit.,* IV, 275.

[100] Canon 2298, 2°; Wernz-Vidal, *op. cit.,* VII, 355; Coronata, *op. cit.,* IV, 270.

[101] Conc. Trident., sess. XXI, *de ref.,* c. 2: ". . . . non decat eos, qui divino ministerio adscripti sunt, cum ordinis dedecore mendicare, aut sordidum aliquem quaestum exercere . . . "

[102] The four general privileges, namely, a) *privilegium canonis* (c. 119), b) *privilegium fori* (c. 120), c) *privilegium immunitatis* (c. 121), and d) *privilegium competentiae* (c. 122), enjoyed by a cleric are conferred on him in recognition of the dignity of the clerical state. No individual cleric can renounce these prvileges, since they are accorded not in consideration of one's personal merit nor by way of reward, but for the benefit of the

What kind of support must a priest receive from an ordinary? Canon 220, § 3,[103] answers this question when it says that an ordinary is bound to provide a respectable support for a cleric who has been deprived of a benefice or a pension which served as a title for his ordination (without prejudice, of course, to the canons 2303 and 2304). This rule of support is also applied to those priests who have been ordained on the title of service of the diocese or of the mission,[104] since clerics ordained on the title of service of the diocese or the mission have the same right of support as clerics ordained on the title of benefice or pensions. Pastors of parishes in the United States of America are considered to have benefices.[105]

Honesta sustentatio[106] is the measure of support in which the ordinary takes care of the needs of a priest in a suitable manner. This support should not consist of a mere pittance. It should be enough to take good care of his ordinary needs, so that he will not be obliged to beg or engage himself in unclerical work for the purpose of supporting himself. A suspended priest still retains membership in the priestly state, enjoys the right of wearing the ecclesiastical garb, and shares in the clerical privileges. Even though a priest has been convicted of a crime, still he is a priest

---

clerical state. Thus, the Church alone can deprive a cleric of these privileges, but always simply for a just cause.

A cleric in virtue of his status in orders and his tenure of an office has also some rights and obligations aside from the general privileges, viz., a priest in good standing has a right to say Mass (cc. 804, 805), and a pastor has the right to baptize his parishioners (c. 462). A cleric for a just cause, however, could be deprived of the exercise of these rights or of his office apart from being deprived of his privileges as a cleric. Thus, a priest who is suspended, v.g., deprived of his income, can still enjoy the privileges of his priestly state.

[103] "Nequit clericus privari beneficio aut pensione cujus titulo ordinatus fuit, nisi aliunde ejus honestae sustentationi provideatur, salvo praescripto can. 2303, 2304." Cf. Prümmer, *Manuale Juris Canonici* (4. et 5. ed., Friburgi Brisgoviae: Herder, 1927), p. 669 (hereafter cited as *Manuale*); Vermeersch-Creusen, *Epitome,* III, p. 300; Coronata, *Institutiones,* IV, p. 259; Augustine, *A Commentary,* VIII, 257, 218.

[104] Cf. Beste, *Introductio,* pp. 228, 714.

[105] Bouscaren, *Law Digest,* I, 150.

[106] Canon 2299.

and should not therefore be left to himself so as to be obliged to beg.[107]

This support should definitely be lower than the fitting maintenance of a priest in good standing or of one who has incurred a lesser vindictive penalty, though on the other hand he should receive more than the support which an ordinary in his charity accords to a deposed cleric.[108] Adequate food, sufficient proper clothing, medical care, books suitable for reading and study, minor and the commonly accepted luxuries such as tobacco and occasional recreation should be included in this subsidy.[109] These things should with greater reason be likewise supplied as they are supplied today in secular penal institutions, though they should not be given in such a generous measure, for an undue generosity would create a semblance of approbation or encouragement of the delinquency.[110]

A local ordinary has no obligation to support a suspended priest if this priest has a patrimony which may have been constituted as his title of ordination. The same may be said of financial assistance derived from membership in a clerical aid society. This is not lost through suspension, unless the by-laws so provide.[111]

In making a provision for this matter the Fathers of a plenary council determine it in the light of all the particular circumstances affecting their own territories both in regard to the ability of their dioceses to provide and in regard to the conditions of the priests. This support should not be tantamount to a pension, for otherwise the penalty of suspension would be rendered illusory inasmuch as the delinquent would obtain a benefit rather than suffer a privation. This has been the common teaching of canonists both before

---

[107] Conc. Trident., sess. XXI, *de ref.*, c. 2. Cf. S. C. de Prop. Fide, instr. 27 apr. 1871: "Cum indecorum omnino sit atque a clericorum qui in sacris Ordinibus constituuntur dignitate prorsus alienum, ut ipsi aut emendicatis subsidiis, aut ex sordido quaestu ea quae ad victum necessaria sunt, sibi comparare cogantur, nemo ignorat."—*Fontes*, n. 4878.

[108] Canon 2303, § 2; Coronata, *Institutiones*, IV, 273.

[109] Smith, *Elements*, III, 95-97.

[110] Sipos, *Enchiridion*, p. 1002.

[111] Cf. Augustine, *A Commentary*, VIII, 260, 261.

and after the Code.[112] The main purpose of this support to a suspended priest is that he be not reduced to abject poverty.

D. Sacred Music

1. Sacred Music in Divine Worship

Liturgical laws regarding sacred music call for due observance.[113] Religious music (which is used in non-liturgical ceremonies) and liturgical music proper have to possess, like all sacred music, the quality of holiness, propriety of form or artistry, and universality. It must be holy because it is designed to express realities whose holiness is supreme; it must be a true specimen of holy art. Every art is designed to express beauty in some form; the beauty which the liturgy must strive to express with the aid of all the arts is God Himself, Who is Beauty, Substantial, Eternal, Infinite.[114] These prerequisites are fully present in Gregorian Chant, which the Church would ever have intimately associated with the Latin words of the sacred liturgy. The proper language of the Church is Latin. Even if the Church has granted certain exceptions from this rule, contrary customs in so far as the use of the vernacular chant is concerned leave unchanged the general norm that the words proper to the liturgy are not to be sung in the vernacular. The Church's great interest in music stems from its close relation to worship. Sacred music, therefore, must conform to the same rules that govern all religious art. The attempt to introduce into churches types of music lacking in any religious inspiration, and to justify this with specious arguments about artistic freedom, is out of place.

The music and its presentation are to be such as would increase the devotion of the faithful. At times the music is good but the

[112] Cf. Wernz, *Ius Decretalium,* VI, 119; 133, note 231; Wernz-Vidal, *Ius Canonicum,* VII, p. 383; Cocchi, *Commentarium,* VIII, 200; Blat, *Commentarium,* VI, 185; Sipos, *Enchiridion,* p. 1002.

[113] Canon 1264, § 1.

[114] Cf. Pius X, motu propr. *Inter pastoralis officii,* 22 nov. 1903—*Fontes,* n. 654. Cf. also Translation of Pius XII's encyclical letter on Sacred Music, *Musicae Sacrae Disciplina,* December 25, 1955 (Washington 5, D. C.: N.C.W.C. News Service), p. 9 (hereafter cited as Ep. encycl. *Musicae Sacrae*).

presentations is such as might befit the stage rather than the Lord's house.[115] Thus it is highly recommended that popular hymns, in order to be acceptable, must fully conform to Christian teachings, have easy words and a simple tune, and possess a certain gravity and dignity. Regarding this matter, St. Pius X stated: "Nothing, therefore, should have place in the temple that is calculated to disturb, or even merely to diminsh, the piety and devotion of the faithful; nothing that may give reasonable cause for disgust or scandal; nothing, above all, which directly offends the decorum and the sanctity of the sacred functions, and is thus unworthy of the House of Prayer and the Majesty of God."[116]

2. Obligation of Pastors

The pastor is the guardian of the music that is presented in the parochial church. A careful and constant guard must be kept over the music that is used lest some lascivious or other improper renditions be given in the House of God.[117] The word "lascivious" here means music that suggests rather the profane than the ecclesiastical ideal.[118] Some discernment is required if one is to adjudge the presence of such a defect in instrumental music. Anyway, among the musical instruments, violins, violas, violincellos, contra-bassos, flutes, bassoons and trumpets are permitted by the Church,[119] but harps, pianos, guitars, zithers, bass drums, triangles, xylophones, trombones,[120] tambourines, castanets, bells, and such like, are excluded,[121] though oboes and clarinets are moderately permitted

---

[115] Cf. Benedictus XIV, ep. encycl. *Annus qui,* 19 febr. 1749—*Fontes,* n. 395.

[116] *Collectanea,* II, n. 2182; Terry, *Catholic Church Music* (London, 1907), p. 9 (hereafter cited as *Church Music*).

[117] Canon 1264, § 1; Conc. Trident., sess. XXII, *decretum de observandis et evitandis in celebratione Missae;* cf. *Collectanea,* II, n. 1621.

[118] Benedictus XIV, ep. encycl. Annus qui, 19 febr. 1749—*Fontes,* n. 395; Terry, *Church Music,* p. 21; Ep. encycl. *Musicae Sacrae,* p. 4, n. 18.

[119] S. R. C., *Compostellana,* 1 apr. 1905—*Decr. Auth. S. R. C.,* n. 4156, ad I.

[120] Romita, *Jus Musicae Sacrae* (Taurini: Marietti, 1936), p. 241.

[121] S. R. C., *Motu Propio SS. D. N. Pii Papae X De Musica Sacra,* 22 nov. 1903—*Decr. Auth. S. R. C.,* n. 4121.

according to the permission of the ordinaries.[122] Chimes and peals played together with the organ for liturgical services are not allowed.[123] The electric organ is not forbidden; local ordinaries may authorize its use.[124]

The Church music, it is true, must be in keeping with the liturgical laws, but this does not mean that Gregorian Chant alone is permissible. Polyphony, which began to come into being in the fourteenth century, when the plain chant commenced to decline, was never condemned by the Church.[125] As a matter of fact, Pius XI reaffirmed the provisions of the Motu Proprio of St. Pius X, and made further recommendations to the bishops for the cultivation of Gregorian Chant and polyphonic music.[126]

The choir, if possible, should be composed of male voices only. The provision in the Motu Proprio of St. Pius X, that women are not to have a part in the strictly liturgical chants of the sacred liturgy (n. 113), has been the most difficult to comply with in many parish churches. Nevertheless, the Sacred Congregation of Rites has since shown the mind of the Holy See to be rather lenient in yielding partly to local customs in this matter, thus a decree addressed to the Most Reverend Archbishop of New York in 1908 permitted women to sing in church choirs, with the provision that women and girl chorists occupy a place separate from that of the men and the boys.[127]

The bishops gathered in a plenary council should promote with every care and every means the singing of popular religious hymns in the dioceses for which the council is being held. That these popular religious songs may be more easily learned and memorized by the faithful, the bishops should establish laws regarding this matter and even form committees for sacred music for the whole territory, if it be necessary. Experienced persons will not be lack-

---

[122] S. R. C., *Compostellana,* 13 nov. 1908—*Decr. Auth. S. R. C.,* n. 4226, ad I.

[123] *AAS,* IX (1917), 352.

[124] AAS, XLI (1949), 617.

[125] Terry, *Church Music,* p. 55; Ep. encycl. *Musicae Sacrae,* p. 3, n. 15.

[126] *AAS,* XXI (1929), 33; cf. Bouscaren, *Law Digest,* I, 598.

[127] S. R. C., *Neo-Eboracen.,* 18 dec. 1908—*Decr. Auth. S. R. C.,* n. 4231; Ep. encycl. *Musicae Sacrae,* p. 17, n. 74.

ing to collect such hymns for the religious training of youth. The Fathers of the council should remember that sacred music will counteract those profane songs which, either through the sentimentality of their tunes or the accompanying lyrics, often voluptuous and lascivious, are usually dangerous to Christians, particularly the youth.

Every pastor should, therefore, read the Motu Proprio of St. Pius X, issued by him on November 22, 1903,[128] and the provisions of the Apostolic Constitution of Pius XI on the Liturgy, the Gregorian Chant, and Sacred Music,[129] in order that he may understand what these Roman Pontiffs of happy memory wanted in regard to church music. Moreover, each pastor should know the new provisions of the recent encyclical, *Musicae Sacrae Disciplina,* issued by Pope Pius XII on December 25, 1955,[130] the application of which, it is earnestly hoped, will find much success.

Finally, these wishes of the Roman Pontiffs will be realized only when the pastors and others who have charge of sacred music will make themselves acquainted with the above-mentioned texts and put their directions into practice. With patience and persevering interest in the ancient solemn and prayerful chants of the Church, the pastors can restore the dignity of Catholic worship.

E. Catholic Schools

Schools may be either private or public. The former are founded and owned by private individuals or groups of individuals, and maintain their character of private institutions even when they are recognized or endowed by public authority. The latter, however, are entirely dependent on public authority, which may be either ecclesiastical or civil, according to whether these schools come under the control of the Church or of the State.[131] An institution,

---

[128] *Fontes,* n. 654; *Pii X Pontificis Maximi Acta* (5 vols., Romae: Ex Typographia Vaticana, 1905-1914, Vol. I, Romae, 1905), I, 75-78; *AAS,* XXXVI (1903-1904), 329-339; 387-395.

[129] *AAS,* XXI (1929), 33 ff.

[130] *The Register* (Denver, Colorado, 1925-), XXXII (1956), n. 6, pp. 8-9.

[131] Cf. Vermeersch-Creusen, *Epitome,* II, n. 709; Wernz, *Ius Decretalium,* III, n. 74; Boffa, *Canonical Provisions for Catholic Schools,* The

however, wherein, under the supervision of the Church, children and youths are trained with a view to cultivating in the light of Christian revelation the higher faculties of the soul—the intellect and the will— is a Catholic school.[132]

1. Establishment of Catholic Schools

The right of both the parents and the State in the establishment of schools is always honored and respected by the Church. The Church does not claim a monopoly of education, nor undertake the foundation of educatioual institutions as long as those schools which are already existing have due regard for the place the Church must have in the schools and in the formation of the Catholic youth.[133] Thus, the obligation imposed by the law[134] is conditional. Whenever Catholic schools do not exist, or when the existing schools present a danger to the faith of Catholic pupils attending them,[135] then the law of the Church is mandatory. At present, prevailing conditions very seldom permit the Church to receive the recognition which it merits in regard to its influence and active participation in the school curricula. Therefore, in these and similar circumstances, the law of establishing Catholic schools under the direct control of the Church becomes mandatory.[136]

The provisions of canon 1379 bear a striking analogy to the situation in the Philippines and in the United States of America, where, because of the strict neutrality of the public school system, the general ecclesiastical law of these countries, as well as the par-

---

Catholic University of America Canon Law Studies, n. 117 (Washington, D. C.: The Catholic University of America Press, 1939), p. 5 (hereafter cited as *Canonical Provisions*).

[132] Demeuran, *L'Eglise-Constitution-Droit Public* (Paris, 1914), p. 197.

[133] Creusen, "L'Ecole Catholique," *Nouvelle Revue Théologique* (Tournai, 1869-), LIII (1926), 193.

[134] Canon 1379, § 1.—Si scholae catholicae ad normam can. 1373 sive elementariae sive mediae desint, curandum, praesertim a locorum Ordinariis, ut condantur.

[135] Canon 1374.

[136] Scharnagl, *Religionsunterricht und Schule nach dem neuen kirchlichen Gesetzbuch* (2. ed., M. Gladbach, 1923, in *Schulpolitik und Erziehung: Zeitfragen,* Heft 15), pp. 21-22 (hereafter cited as *Religionsunterricht*); De Luca, *Institutiones Iuris Publici Ecclesiastici* (2 vol., Romae, 1904), II, 229.

ticular laws of each diocese, have recognized the necessity of establishing Catholic schools at any reasonable cost. Since the laws of these two countries basically respect the right of both individuals and families, the Church has ample opportunity to estabilsh schools so that parents may send their children to institutions of their own choice.[137]

The Fathers of the II Plenary Council of Baltimore (1866), after declaring that experience had proved that attendance at public schools constituted a great danger to the faith and morals of Catholic children, concluded that the establishment of parochial schools was the necessary remedy.[138] The Fathers of the Provincial Council of Manila in 1910 likewise insisted on the necessity of parochial schools.[139] Furthermore, the Fathers of the III Plenary Council of Baltimore (1884) issued the following command regarding the establishment of parochial schools:

> Prope unamquamque ecclesiam ubi nondum existit, scholam parochialem intra duos annos a promulgatione hujus Concilii erigendam . . . esse, nisi Episcopus ob graviores difficultates concedendam esse judicet.[140]

These decrees are more detailed than the Code, but in no wise opposed to it, and therefore continue to have their full force. They are incorporated into diocesan statutes,[141] and form the general law regulating the establishment of parochial schools in the diocese.

---

[137] Lischka, *Private Schools and State Laws* (Washington: The National Catholic Welfare Conference, 1926), p. 186; *Constitution of the Republic of the Philippines,* art. III, sect. 1 (6); cf. Sinco, *Philippine Government and Political Law* (5. ed., Manila: Community Publishers, 1949), p. 324; Coquia, *Legal Status of the Church in the Philippines* (Washington, D. C.: The Catholic University of America Press, 1950), p. 122.

[138] *Conc. Plen. Baltim. II, Acta et Decreta,* n. 430.

[139] *Concilio de Manila,* n. 826.

[140] *Conc. Plen. Baltim. III, Acta et Decreta,* n. 199.

[141] Cf.. ex. gr., *Constituciones del Seguido Sínodo de Lipa* (1944), cap. XXXIV, art. 369, (b); *Fourth Diocesan Synod of Lafayette, La.* (1953), tit. XVI, n. 277; *Statutes of the Archdiocese of Dubuque* (1947), art. 22, n. 349.

2. Danger of Non-Catholic Schools

The term non-Catholic schools (*schola acatholica*) could be considered either in a general sense or in a specific one. One could consider that a school is non-Catholic when it does not impart any Catholic education or training, and this is the general sense, which would include institutions of a neutral, mixed and lay character. In the other sense, it means either an anti-Catholic school (one opposed to Catholic principles) or a non-Catholic school, whether it propounds a heretical, a schismatic or a pagan religion. The Code uses the term *acatholica* in the latter sense, because it distinguishes non-Catholic schools from schools of a neutral or also a mixed character. Thus, the two latter classes must not be understood as being mentioned in the Code merely by way of example.[142]

In many localities neutral schools are commonly called "public." At present, in almost every country, this type of school is increasing. Its goal is concerned with the temporal end of man to the exclusion of any and every specific religious tenet. Another name for neutral schools is "lay," i.e., it designates an institution that is independent of ecclesiastical authority, in regard both to its teaching and to its personnel, but "lay" and "neutral" are not interchangeable.[143] A lay school is not agnostic, nor is it silent in the face of spiritual problems. On the contrary, it opens the way to a free discussion of any religious, moral or philosophical question. Without teaching one religion rather than another, it puts all religions before the eyes of the student, cultivates in the pupil a critical sense, so as to help him think for himself in a way supposedly more fitting to his undividual mind and conscience. Neutral schools are in reality centers of religious indifferentism that prove dangerous to Catholic youth, a fact duly noted by the Sovereign Pontiffs.[144]

---

[142] Cf. Schmid, "De vi verborum 'acatholicus, secta acatholica, minister acatholicus' in Jure Canonico," *Apollinaris,* IV (1931), 559.

[143] Cf. Najera, *Derecho Docente de la Iglesia, la Familia y el Estado* (Linares: Impr. "El Noticiero," 1934), p. 325 (hereafter cited as *Derecho Docente*); Boffa, *Canonical Provisions,* p. 109.

[144] Leo XIII, ep. encycl. *Nobilissima,* 8 febr. 1884, n. 4—*Fontes,* n. 590; Pius XI, litt. encycl. *Divini illius Magistri,* 31 dec. 1929—*AAS,* XXII (1930), 76-77.

In a school of mixed character the youth of both sexes are admitted, and in this case such a school is called a coeducational institution. In a mixed school as in a neutral school the children of any religious denomination are admitted, though, in the former, religious instruction is imparted as a unit of the school curriculum, and is taught separately according to the different beliefs of the pupils. It often happens however that tenets common to all religions are taught indiscriminately to the students. In the Code, mixed schools are those which admit pupils of any and also of no religion.[145] Catholic schools, however, even though they admit some non-Catholic pupils, do not come under this classification.

The Church forbids attendance at these various schools, because it finds in them a danger to the faith of its children. These dangers may exist by reason either of the curriculum or of the promiscuous association with students of so many different faiths.

In fact, the curriculum of these schools presents a constant danger to the faith of the Catholic youth, because, if the curriculum is devoid of all religious instruction, the pupil is also deprived of knowledge most necessary for life, without which one cannot live in a Christian manner.[146] Besides, if all religious doctrines are presented indiscriminately, the result for the student will most frequently be an attitude of indifferentism. Lastly, if religious doctrine is taught but is separated from the rest of the curriculum, the pupil is not likely to set a just value on its practical significance in life, but will consider it rather as a speculative problem.

The daily intimate companionship of Catholic youth with those of other beliefs or of no faith whatsoever militates against the security of the faith of the Catholic children. The outcome of this constant comradeship often reflects a pattern of non-Catholic thinking, which imbues the minds of Catholic youth with error, or, to say the least, with indifferentism. It is in the light of these dangers that one must measure the strength of the prohibition of the Church regarding non-Catholic schools.

The Popes, particularly Pope Leo XIII, recommended the estab-

---

145 Canon 1374.

146 S. C. S. Off., instr. (ad Ep. Stat. Foeder, Americae Septentrion.), 24 nov. 1875—*Fontes*, n. 1046.

lishment of Catholic schools as the most proper means of neutralizing the dangers of non-Catholic schools for the Catholic youth. On Nov. 17, 1885, he expressed full appreciation to the English Bishops for their zeal in establishing schools.[147] In a letter to the Bishops of Bavaria, he said: "We have had many noble examples of religious generosity from Catholics who have established and maintained, with the greatest burden and expense, schools of their own religious conviction in those places where only neutral schools exist. It is to be fervently hoped that these glorious and secure asylmus for the youth will be established in larger numbers as circumstances and local conditions allow."[148]

Finally, the zeal of the American episcopacy in establishing schools in every parish, and the endeavors of the Dutch hierarchy who, after long and difficult controversies, have gained a juridical and financial equality for their schools as compared with the schools of the State, are well known.[149]

3. Support of Catholic Schools

It is true that to erect and maintain schools is not the concern of the Church alone. In localities where there are no suitable Catholic schools, however, it becomes necessary for the Church to establish schools of its own, and, if this is a duty of the Church, then in justice it is also the duty of its members to support these schools. This obligation rests on every member of the Church's society. It is not the obligation of parents alone who have children in such schools, though they make use in a more direct manner of the privileges of sending their children to such schools, but it is the obligation of every member of the Church as well,[150] since Catholic schools affect the whole Christian community, and serve a common purpose.

Since a good moral and Christian education is of the greatest

---

[147] *ASS*, XVIII (1885-1886), 305.

[148] Ep. *Officio Sanctissimo*, 22 dec. 1887, n. 9—*Fontes*, n. 596.

[149] Cf. *Das holländische Schulgesetz* (Düsseldorf, 1921)—*Schulpolitik und Erziehung*: Zeitfragen, Heft 11; Scharnagl, *Religionsunterricht*, pp. 21-22.

[150] *Acta et Decreta Conc. Plen. Quebecensis Primi, Anno Domini MCMIX* (Quebeci: Typis "L'Action Sociale Limitée," 1912), n. 287 d.

importance to the well-being of society at large,[151] and since the purpose of society is to procure and foster a constant betterment, both material and spiritual, of the families composing it, the obligation of supporting Catholic schools rests also on the State, especially when it professes the Catholic faith. It is the duty of the State either to establish Catholic schools, or, if this is not feasible on account of the different faiths of its citizens, at least to contribute proportionately to the support of these schools.[152]

Catholic schools, in educating children who are both citizens and members of the society in which they live, are entitled in justice to a proportionate share in the money which is allotted for public education. The State commits a serious offense against distributive justice at large every time it refuses to render support to Catholic schools or to contribute proportionately, and makes provision for public instruction solely by means of a neutral or mixed school system, proposing at the same time that everyone who wants an education at public expense must make use of these schools.[153] Such is the case in the Philippines and in the United States of America, where Catholics are confronted with a double burden in order to give a proper education to their children. It is to be hoped that Catholics in these two countries will be given a fair and just recognition in this matter.[154]

How much must the faithful give for the support of Catholic schools? The Code does not specify any amount in this regard. It

---

[151] Cf. Leo XIII, litt. encycl. *Sapientiae,* 10 ian. 1890, n. 2—Fontes, 605; Pius XI, litt. encycl. *Divini illius Magistri,* 31 dec. 1929—*AAS,* XXII (1930), 51.

[152] Ottaviani, *Institutiones,* II, 245; cf. art. 6 of the Concordat with Bavaria—*AAS,* XVII (1925), 45; art. 23 of the Concordat with Germany—*AAS,* XXV (1933), 402; art. 6, § 4, of the Concordat with Austria—*AAS,* XXVI (1934), 257; Restrepo, *Concordata regnante Sanctissimo Domino Pio PP. XI Inita* (Romae: Apud Aedes Pont. Universitatis Gregorianae, 1934), p. 636, note 547.

[153] Pius XI, litt. encycl. *Divini illius Magistri,* 31 dec. 1929—*AAS,* XXII (1930), 78; Monti, La Libertà della Scuola (Milano: Soc. Ed. "Vita e Pensiero," 1928), pp. 61-64.

[154] Gabel, *Public Funds for Church and Private Schools* (Toledo, 1937), pp. 750-779.

simply reminds the faithful of their obligation, and insists that they contribute to the best of their ability.[155] It is often really difficult to convince the faithful about their obligation to support these institutions. In general, the attitude of those who benefit directly from these schools is very co-operative. Not everybody, however, has this willingness to co-operate, and the taking up of extra collections often becomes a continual source of irritation. Thus some suggestions regarding this matter may prove somewhat helpful.

First of all, there is the admirable practice in certain communities of organizing in each parish some kind of society, the purpose of which is the soliciting of financial contributions, so that the parochial schools may be rendered free of charge for the pupils attending them.[156] With regard to the support of schools of higher education, a general formation of endowment funds could probably bring a happy solution.[157] A discreet exercise of the franchise system could provide another way of maintenance, since Catholics, as citizens, might bring influence to gear on the public authority to establish Catholic schools or, if already established, to make an equitable contribution towards their support. Under a democratic form of government this is not impossible, for even though the government does not profess the Catholic religion, yet much of the action of its legislature is influenced by the vote of the citizens.[158]

There are other various ways by which Catholics can contribute to the support of their schools. The local ordinaries, on whom the obligation of establishing Catholic schools rests primarily, are the best judges to determine what kind of method is most appropriate for this purpose. When these local ordinaries are gathered in a

---

[155] Canon 1379, § 3: Fideles ne ommittant adiutricem operam pro viribus conferre in catholicas scholas . . . sustentandas.

[156] *Acta et Decreta Conc. Plen. Baltim.* III, n. 202.

[157] Kremer, *Church Support in the United States,* The Catholic University of America Canon Law Studies, n. 61 (Washington, D. C.: The Catholic University of America, 1930), pp. 61-69; Boffa, *Canonical Provisions,* p. 148.

[158] Coronata, *Institutiones,* II, 305; Michel, *La Question Scolaire et les Principes Théologiques* (Paris: Desclée, De Brouwer, 1921), p. 131, note 2.

plenary council they should consider which method is preferable and fitting for the particular circumstances and needs in their respective territories.

4. Pastors and Their Duties

The Code of Canon Law enumerates among the duties of pastors that of particular vigilance lest in the public and private schools in their parishes anything be taught which does not correspond to Catholic faith and morals.[159] They are to see that the "purity of faith and morals be preserved among the laity," and that "in schools, both for children and youth, the training be in conformity with the principles of the Catholic religion."[160] This vigilance is a part of the care of souls. It touches more or less directly anyone who is connected with this ministry. This right of vigilance in relation to secular matters in the schools is in itself of a negative nature. It empowers the holder to see that nothing take place which, in any way, is contrary to Catholic faith and morals. From the pedagogical point of view, however, vigilance includes an intervention in school affairs which extends to the whole routine of the schools and affects both teachers and pupils.

Another obligation of pastors is that of founding Catholic schools. Although this obligation falls directly on the local ordinaries and particularly on the residential bishops, they being the proper and immediate pastors of the dioceses entrusted to them,[161] nevertheless the pastors themselves must also exert their highest diligence in the Catholic education of children.[162] To this effect Pope Leo XIII approved the decree of the Plenary Council of Latin America which stated: "In order to facilitate the grave obligation resting on Catholic parents concerning the education of their children, we command all pastors to found, either through themselves or others, elementary schools in their parishes when-

[159] Canon 469.

[160] Cf. S. C. C., *Conimbricen.*, 18 aug., 1 sept. 1888—*ASS,* XXI (1898), 686.

[161] Canon 334, § 1.

[162] Canon 467, § 1.—Debet parochus . . . maximam curam adhibere in catholica puerorum institutione.

even none exist. This is to be done in so far as the bishop will judge it possible, and at the time and in the manner established by him."[163]

Pastors should not regard the parish schools as a place to work in, but as a place to work with. The parochial school is a bulwark of Christianity which the Church uses for its perpetuation. The pastors must consider well that Catholic schools give their students a complete training in order to enable these students to defend the Church, in later years, against the unjust attacks of its opponents, and to repel those influences which will bear upon them in an attempt to rob them of their God and their religion. These are the reasons why every pastor should strive to have a parochial school in his parish.

5. Obligation of Parents

The term "parents" means fathers and mothers, i.e., those who beget children by physical generation, whether legitimately in marriage or illicitly outside of wedlock. Hence parents of illegitimate children, natural or spurious, are obliged to provide for the religious and moral instruction of their offspring, just the same as those who are legitimately married. As a matter of fact, the education of the children is as primary a purpose of marriage as is their procreation.[164]

One of the prerogatives of the Church is the right to determine the duties of parents regarding the religious and moral training of their children. The Church does not intrude upon any matter of a strictly profane nature. It has, nevertheless, an indirect authority over such matters in so far as they relate to spiritual issues and involve a moral content. Thus, in all that relates to the supernatural order or pertains to it, the Church has a right to govern, and the parents may well in such matters be said to be its delegates and instruments in the performance of its work for the salvation of souls.[165] The Church, therefore, forbids parents to send their

---

[163] *Acta et Decreta Concilii Plenarii Americae Latinae* (1899), p. 678.

[164] Canon 1013, § 1. Cf. Gredt, *Elementa Philosophiae Aristotelico-Thomisticae* (7. ed., 2 vol., Friburgi Brisgoviae: Herder, 1937), II, n. 1017.

[165] Capello, *Summa Iuris Publici Ecclesiastici* (3. ed., Romae: Apud

children to any schools but those which are Catholic, except in cases in which the bishop of the diocese judges that attendance at another school may be allowed without danger to the children's faith.[166]

The Church, in its consistent conviction that intellectual, moral and religious training cannot be separated from one another without harm to the pupils makes it its law that every Catholic school must include religious training.[167] Thus, parents who are bound to educate their children for the correct performance of their duties, for the enjoyment of happiness in this world, and for the attainment of their destiny in the world to come, must send their children to Catholic schools in addition to supporting such institutions.

6. Influence of Teachers

Since teachers inevitably exercise an influence over the pupils because of the very close association existing between them and the pupils whom they teach,[168] it is but congruous that the teachers possess firm religious convictions which both regulate and reflect their lives. Even in the case of sincere and thoroughly Catholic teachers there is need of authoritative direction and control. If the authority of the Church is denied, there is no longer any guarantee that a teacher will remain within the limits of orthodoxy. His personal sentiments, though inspired by the best intentions, may lead him to ambiguity, exaggerations, and even to error in the teaching and the application of truths, which partly at least in their very import surpass human understanding. Thus, it is prudent that non-Catholic teachers be not admitted in Catholic schools, for fear that they influence their pupils according to their way of thinking, and thus imbue the minds of the pupils with error, or, to say the least, with indifferentism. "One must be a novice in human affairs," wrote the Holy Office, "if one does not see the dangers which

---

Aedes Universitatis Gregorianae, 1932), p. 505. Cf. Godts, *Les Droits en Matière d'Education* (5 vols., Bruxelles, 1900-1901), IV, 858.

[166] Canon 1374.

[167] Canon 1373.

[168] Casotti, *Maestro e Scolaro—Saggio di Filosofia dell'Educazione* (Milano: Soc. Ed. "Vita e Pensiero," 1930), p. 17; Boffa, *Canonical Provisions*, p. 110.

teachers not of the fold bring into the classroom. In season and out of season they take every possible occasion to circumvent the simplicity of youth and to bend it, so to speak, into conformity with their tenets; their schemes becoming even more efficacious the more secret they are."[169]

If possible, Sisters should be procured to be the teachers in Catholic schools, especially in parochial schools. The influence they have upon the children is so great that it cannot be denied. It is true that every woman has a right to reverence, but how much more is this true regarding the teaching Sisters. "They are," as Sacerdos writes in the American Ecclesiastical Review, "the chosen souls of the Most High, the spouses of Christ, the King; they have left all that is dear to the human heart to follow the call of the Heavenly Bridegroom. They have bound themselves by the strongest ties to a special union with Christ, and Him they are following in the godly work of leading the little ones to their Master. The zeal and fervor with which they are performing their arduous duties, may well compel the admiration of us priests and make us blush for our shortcomings. Ah! these wonderful nuns! the glorious vivandières in the march of the army of Christ! No stars bedeck them, nor crosses; no poet sings of them; no trumpets blare round their rough and toilsome march and struggle; but some day the bede-roll will be called, and the King's right hand will pin on their breasts the cross of His Legion of Honor."[170]

F. Censure and Prohibition of Books

The duty of the Church to exercise censorship arises primarily from the teaching magisterium of the Church. The Code itself places the canons on the censorship and prohibition of books under the general heading of the teaching magisterium of the Church.[171]

The divine mission of the Church is to guide men to their eternal salvation. The Church cannot accomplish this mission on earth by offering merely its sacraments to the faithful and instructing them in the body of its doctrine and in its code of morals; it needs

[169] S.S.C. Off., instr. 21 mart. 1866—*Fontes,* n. 992.

[170] Vol. LVII (1917), 13.

[171] Canons 1384-1405.

also to preserve them from erroneous doctrines and evil practices. Thus, the censorship and prohibiton of books are both useful and necessary in the realm of the printed word.

Every legitimate society has the natural right to ward off anything that may endanger the moral and physical welfare of its subjects, and to protect these subjects from harm. As the Church is a legitimate society with subjects for whom is responsible within its own sphere, it cannot be destitute of the authority and the power which will enable it to keep its subjects uncontaminated and free from harm. Of all the dangers that imperil man's salvation, bad literature is perhaps the most destructive. Hence there arises the right of the Church to control the reading of its children by requiring that certain books be submitted for official examination and approval before publication (censorship), and the right to prohibit the publication, reading, retention, sale or communication of bad books (prohibition of books).

1. Censorship

It is a well known fact attested by history that the Catholic Church has always claimed to be appointed by Christ as the sole guardian and authorized teacher and interpreter of the religious truths taught by Christ.[172] The State has the right of censorship regarding those matters which are necessary for the temporal end of the state.[173] In any event, at least in Christian countries, the civil government cannot independently of the Church exercise such a right regarding books dealing with religion.[174] The right belongs also to the heads of families with regard to those who are subject to them.[175] The right of the Church to lead its sheep upon wholesome pastures and to point out the poisonous weeds that endanger the welfare of its children requires both repressive and preventive remedies, which the Church is certainly permitted to apply in teaching and preserving the deposit of faith.

[172] Cf. canon 1322, § 1.

[173] Cavagnis, *Institutiones Iuris Publici Ecclesiastici* (4. ed., 3 vols., Romae: Desclée, Lefebvre, et Soc., 1906), I, n. 122.

[174] Cf. Wernz, *Ius Decretalium,* III, nn. 99, 103.

[175] Cf. De Meester, *Compendium,* III, Pars I, n. 1335.

One of these remedies is the censorship of books. Censorship is the name given to the judgment rendered by any ecclesiastical authority in certifying that a certain book contains no apparent conflict with the faith.[176] Thus, censorship protects the deposit of faith and the morality of the faithful.

The Church has always exercised this power of censorship in various ways and with different methods according to the exigencies of different times.[177] From the very beginning, the Church accepted books at their true value. It is obviously known that the Church made a wise use of good books, just the same as it dealt severely with pernicious ones. The Apostles frequently warned the faithful against the harmful influence of a very intimate association with the enemies of Christianity either in word or in writing.[178] The incident involving Paul at Ephesus is but the first in a long chain.[179]

At first, the procedure of censorship was enforced locally, and the first laws requiring the approval of books appeared in Germany at the end of the fourteenth century.[180] Within a few decades, however, the popes extended this legislation to the entire Church, and the first general law was enacted in the V general Council of the Lateran.[181] Later on, this initial universal legislation was reenacted and integrated by the Council of Trent.[182] Afterwards, Pope Leo XIII, whose legislation was promulgated in the Constitution *Officium ac Munerum,* dated January 25, 1897,[183] modernized completely the law on censorship. This constitution abrogated express-

---

[176] Abbo-Hannan, *The Sacred Canons,* II, 615.

[177] Hurley, *A Commentary on the Present Index Legislation* (Dublin, 1908), p. 23.

[178] I Tim., 6:20; II Tim., 2:16.

[179] Acts, 19:19-20.

[180] Hilgers, *Der Index der verbotenen Bücher* (Freiburg im Breisgau, 1904), p. 404.

[181] Leo X Const. *Inter sollicitudiness,* 4 maii 1515, §§ 2, 3—*Fontes,* n. 68. Cf. Wiest, *Precensorship of Books,* The Catholic University of America Canon Law Studies, n. 329 (Washington 17, D. C.: The Catholic University of America Press, 1953), p. 19 (hereafter cited as *Precensorship*).

[182] Conc. Trident., sess. IV, *de editione et usu sacrorum librorum;* Wiest, *Precensorship,* pp. 20, 21.

[183] *Fontes,* n. 632.

ly all former laws on censorship, except what was enacted in the Constitution *Sollicita et provida* of Benedict XIV.

The right of censorship is so extensive and all-inclusive that the Church could demand censorship of all writings, although actually it does not use its right to the fullest extent. Its right of censorship affects only certain matters, certain persons and certain functions. Certain fields, v.g., writings on profane topics, are completely free of censorship. Since this is a question of positive law, all that is not mentioned either explicitly or implicitly in the law is free from censorship.[184] *De facto* this is a limited freedom of the press. *De iure,* however, there can be no absolute freedom of the press for Catholics,[185] for the law of censorship binds all the faithful, that is, those baptized persons who are members of the Church. It is probable that those baptized persons who are not members of the Church are not obliged by the law.

It had happened frequently that books, though published with the requisite permission of the ordinaries, later were forbidden or withdrawn from circulation by some decree of the Holy Office.[186] The explanation of these happenings could be multiple, but the principal one is the lack of principles employed in the examination of a work. The celebration of a plenary council would be an opportune time for the local ordinaries to make pertinent legislation and to establish the principles that could serve as a guide to all diocesan censors. It is true that censors are to judge a work not according to their private opinions nor in the light of the tenets of a favorite school, but according to the common doctrine of the Church. After a thorough consideration and deliberation concerning the norms to be followed in the censure and prohibition of books, it may earnestly be hoped that all diocesan censors will be both efficient and competent in making correct judgments, whether favorable or unfavorable, in their examination and judgment of books. Thus a uniformity in the practice of censorship can emerge.

---

[184] Goodwine, "Problem Respecting the Censorship of Books," *The Jurist* (Washington, D. C., 1941-), X (1950), 157, (8).

[185] *Ibidem,* p. 153, (4).

[186] *AAS,* XXXIII (1941), 121; Bouscaren, *Law Digest,* II, 436.

2. Prohibition

The right and duty to prohibit books for a good reason is vested not only in the Supreme Pontiff for the universal Church, but also in the particular councils[187] for their respective subjects.[188] As it is very difficult for the Sacred Congregation to stop pernicious books as promptly as possible, and since a good deal of time elapses in some cases before a book is brought to the attention of the Holy See, the help of particular councils is sought by the Code.[189] The Holy See has repeatedly urged the bishops to watch over the the books published in their respective territories and to prohibit those which they find dangerous to Catholic faith and morality.[190]

The prohibition of books is an act of jurisdictional authority. To read certain immoral or harmful books is absolutely prohibited to the faithful in consequence of the Church's jurisdictional authority.[191] This prohibition includes also the publishing, reading, retaining, sending, translating or communicating of the books to others in any manner.[192] The condemnation of books and publications as effected by the Holy Office, inasmuch as it pertains both to discipline and to doctrine, is binding on the Churches of the Oriental Rites.[193] Since the Code states that the prohibition of particular councils affects their respective subjects only, accordingly exempt religious and persons who have not a domicile or a quasi-domicile in the territory for which the plenary council is being held are not bound by its legislation, nor are the subjects bound during their absence from the territory.[194]

It cannot be denied that the evil effects of bad books are diffused from one place to another. Hence some sepecific legislation respecting vigilance, common counsel and united action, which can be

---

[187] V. g., the plenary council.

[188] Cf. canon 1395, § 1.

[189] Sacred Congregation of the Index, Aug. 24, 1864—*Collectanea*, I, n. 1261.

[190] *Loc. cit.*

[191] Wernz-Vidal, *Ius Canonicum*, IV, Pars II, 153.

[192] Canon 1398, § 1; Vermeersch-Creusen, *Epitome*, II, 572.

[193] S. C. Eccl. Or., 26 maii 1928—*AAS*, XX (1928), 195.

[194] Cf. canon 13.

provided efficiently by the plenary council, is obviously needed. Recourse against the legislation of the plenary council may be interposed with the Holy See, but not with a suspensive effect, i.e., the prohibition must be obeyed until Rome has rescinded the orders of the plenary council.[195]

---

[195] Canon 1395, § 2.—Ab hac prohibitione datur ad Sanctam Sedem recursus, non tamen in suspensivo.

CHAPTER VI

Authority of the Conciliar Decrees

Article 1. Recognition of the Conciliar Decrees

Can. 291.—§ 1. Absoluto Concilio plenario . . . praeses acta et decreta omnia ad Sanctam Sedem transmittat, nec eadem antea promulgentur, quam a Sacra Congregatione Concilii expensa et recognita fuerint. . . .

The law states that before the promulgation of conciliar acts and decrees they must be examined by the Sacred Congregation of the Council for recognition. These acts and decrees must bear the signatures of all the Fathers of the council. Even those members who in the deliberations voted in the dissenting minority must affix their signatures to the decrees, since the enactments will have force in the whole territory.[1] This practice of submitting conciliar decrees to the recognition of the Holy See is not very recent, it became a part of the universal law of the Church in the year 1588.[2]

The Holy See gives recognition to the decrees of plenary councils in three ways. They are a) *simplex recognitio;* b) *confirmatio in forma communi,* and c) *confirmatio in forma specifica.*[3] The first way is the usual form of recognition, which consists simply in the inspection of the acts and their correction, whenever this is necessary, but no positive sanction is superadded to them. The second way declares that nothing censurable was found in the acts of the council. This declaration gives the conciliar decrees an additional extrinsic authority, but not any added intrinsic authority. They remain conciliar acts, not papal enactments. Thus, the common impression that in virtue of the examination made by the Holy See the laws become "papal" or "Roman" is erroneous. Even

[1] Cocchi, *Commentaria,* III, 135; Fagnanus, *Commentaria,* Lib. V, tit. 1, cap. 25, n. 94.

[2] Sixtus V, const. *Immensa aeterni, Bull. Rom.,* VIII, 991.

[3] Abbo-Hannan, *The Sacred Canons,* I, 332; Coronata, *Institutiones,* II, 432.

laudatory expressions in the decree of recognition do not change the conciliar enactments into papal laws. Moreover, as this approbation is merely conditional, it presupposes that there is no enactment contrary to the Code or Apostolic Constitutions. Should any of these decrees be opposed to the common law, they would lack juridical force, in spite of the fact that they were officially supervised. Such decrees, therefore, would not be validated by recognition.[4] In every case such invalidity needs to be proved; it can never simply be presumed.[5] The third way is the positive form of approval. It is given *motu proprio* and *ex certa scientia.* It confers on the conciliar acts the authority of papal enactments. The approval given *in forma specifica* is generally expressed in the document of approbation, or else the printed acts and decrees contain the formula, *ex plenitude potestatis approbamus.*[6] Inasmuch as this kind of recognition is not ordinarily given, and since the Code uses the terms *expensa* and *recognita,* this third way of confirmation is not used in the accorded recognition of the decrees of a plenary council. Besides, the Holy See has declared that its confirmation adds no positive approval to the decrees, but is simply a condition of legitimate promulgation.[7]

The statutes are examined by one consultor, then by a commission of consultors, and finally by the Cardinals of the Congregation.[8] This examination is called a *correctio et censura,*[9] and it is done with a view to testing the validity of the acts and decrees

[4] In 1924, in China, a provincial council was held which incorporated a point on implicit dispensation which proved to be at variance with the present practice of the Holy Office. The decrees of the council were confirmed but eight years afterwards, The Holy Office ordered that the decree in question should be corrected. Cf. Sartori, *Enchiridion Canonicum* (3. ed., emendata et aucta, Hankow: Missio Catholica, 1932), p. 146; Bouscaren, *Law Digest,* II, 291, 292; ibidem, I, 512, 513; Hanrahan, "The Law on Plenary Councils," *The Clergy Review,* XIV (1938), 387-402; "From Foreign Reviews," *The Clergy Review,* XIV, 1938), 89, 90.

[5] Coronata, *Compendium Iuris Canonici ad Usum Scholarum* (3 vols., Taurini: Marietti, 1949-1950; Vol. I, 5. ed., 1950; Vol. II, 4. ed., 1950, Vol. III, 1949), I, p. 371, footnote No. 4 (hereafter cited as *Compendium*).

[6] Augustine, *A Commentary,* II, 306.

[7] *AAS,* XIII (1921), 228.

[8] Coronata, *Compendium,* I, p. 371.

[9] Vermeersch-Creusen, *Epitome,* I, n. 360.

of the council, to weighing their wisdom and prudence, and to making any corrections which may be desirable. In general, a few changes are made in the cause of the examination, and expression is given to this with the phrase *"nonnullis tamen ememdationibus inductis."*[10] In case the Sacred Congregation makes any addition to the submitted legislation, the decrees do not suffer any intrinsic change. Any correction made by the Sacred Congregation does not give to the decrees any pontifical authority, nor any positive ratification.[11] From what has been said, it can be seen that there is a clear distinction between papal laws and those of a plenary council. The distinction is not merely a speculative one, for it influences the law on the dispensations that may later have to be granted.[12] Furthermore, the recognition gives to the decrees an added importance and solemnity. It also promotes their ready acceptance and prompt execution among the clergy and the laity.[13]

The Sacred Congregation for the Propagation of the Faith is competent for the examination and the inspection of the acts and decrees of councils held in mission territories, as the Sacred Congregation of the Council is competent for those territories which are subject to the Sacred Consistorial Congregation.[14] The appraisal of the proceedings and enactments by either of these two Congregations, as the case may be, constitutes an additional safeguard in the framing of a uniform law in various ecclesiastical provinces and regions throughout the Catholic world.

---

[10] *AAS,* XV (1923), 454.

[11] "Namque approbatio Sanctae Sedis quae mere conditio est legitimae promulgationis, nullam positivam Sanctae Sedis auctoritatem ad ista decreta superaddit."—S.S.C., 19 febr, 1921—*AAS,* XIII (1921), 228.

[12] Canon 82.—Episcopi aliique locorum Ordinarii dispensare valent in legibus dioecesanis, et in legibus Concilii provincialis ac plenarii ad normam can. 291, § 2, non vero in legibus quas speciatim tulerit Romanus Pontifex pro illo peculiari territorio, nisi ad normam can. 81.

[13] Wernz-Vidal, *Ius Canonicum,* II, 684.

[14] Coronata, *Institutiones,* I, p. 432 in notis n. 2; Abbo-Hannan, *The Sacred Canons,* I, 332; cf. canons 250, § 4; 252, § 2; 304, § 2.

Article 2. Promulgation of the Decrees

Can. 291.—§ 1. Absoluto Concilio plenario . . . ipsimet autem Concilii Patres designent et modum promulgationis decretorum et tempus quo decreta promulgata obligare incipiant.

The juridic efficacy of a law comes from the public manifestation of the legislator's will to the community.[15] As a law is not simply a plan or a norm which exists in the mind of the legislator, but rather a rule of action for the community, it must be made manifest to the community by the authority of him who has the power to impose such a rule of activity, or by another who has his authentic mandate.[16] Since a law is intended not only for a few but for the whole community, it would not be sufficient for the legislator to intimate his will to certain individuals only.[17] Promulgation, therefore, is the authentic publication intimated to a community for which the law is made.[18] The very nature of a law involves the absolute necessity of the promulgation of it. Thus, there is no law and therefore no obligation before a law is promulgated;[19] hence, *"leges instituuntur, cum promulgantur."*[20]

Under the former discipline the Apostolic Legate promulgated the decrees of the plenary council, and such decrees obtained the force of law at once unless other provision was made. The present legislation leaves it to the Fathers of the council to determine the manner of promulgating the decrees duly recognized by the Congregation of the Council and to fix the time when they will gain their juridic force.[21]

Similar to the diocesan statutes, which begin to bind immediately after their promulgation, unless a contrary provision is

---

[15] Michiels, *Normae Generales Juris Canonici* (ed. altera, penitus retractata et notabiliter aucta, 2 vols., Tournai (Belg.): Desclée & Co., 1949), I, 185 (hereafter cited as *Normae Generales*).

[16] Michiels, *Normae Generales,* I, 188.

[17] Benedictus XIV, *De Synodo,* Lib. XIII, cap. 4, n. 1; Van Hove, *Commentarium Lovaniense in Codicem Iuris Canonici* (1 vol. in 5 tomes, Tom. II, *De Legibus Ecclesiasticis,* Mechliniae: H. Dessain, 1930), II, *De Legibus Ecclesiasticis,* 134 (hereafter cited as *De Legibus*).

[18] Michiels, *Normae Generales,* I, 183; Van Hove, *De Legibus,* 112.

[19] Van Hove, *De Legibus,* 115.

[20] Canon 8, § 1.

[21] Canon 291, § 1.

specified,[22] the promulgated laws can begin to oblige either at once[23] or after a short interval of time according to the judgment of the Fathers.[24]

Before the Code, these decrees were to be promulgated in their diocesan synods by the individual bishop within six months.[25] There were also instances, however, when the promulgation was made outside the diocesan synods.[26] Hence the promulgation of the conciliar decrees within diocesan synods or provincial councils is not a requirement of the law.[27] The publication of the decrees in

---

[22] Canon 335, § 2.

[23] Cf. decree of promulgation, I Plenary Council of Quebec (1909): "Omnia et singula, quae in Concilio Plenario decreta et sancita sunt, pro necessitatibus Ecclesiae et salute animarum nostris in regionibus, filiali reverentia et obsequentissimo animo Apostolicae Sedi submittimus. Quia vero nulla lex vim obligandi habere potest nisi promulgetur, statuimus, ut postquam a Sancta Sede decreta hujus Concilii expensa et recognita fuerint, statim promulgentur.

Ne autem ullus supersit dubitandi locus de tempore, quo incipiet obligatio suscipiendi et exsequendi decreta Concilii hujus Plenarii Quebecensis Primi, et ne qua obtendi possit excusatio ob negligentiam vel moram, si qua fuerit, in iisdem per singulas provincias et dioeceses promulgandis, declaramus et omnibus notum facimus cuncta et singula, quae in hoc Concilio Plenario Quebecensi Primo decreta et constituta sunt, vim suam habere plenariosque et integros effectus sortiri per universas hujus religionis ecclesias, statim ac per Reverendissimum Delegatum Apostolicum promulgata fuerint, quin opus sit ea denuo in synodis provincalibus aut dioecesanis promulgare." —*Acta et Decreta Concilii Plenarii Quebecensis Primii* (1909), pp. 481-482.

[24] Cf. can. 5, I Plenary Council of India (1940): Statuimus hujus Concilii decreta quae vim legis habent, tribus mensibus post legitimam eorum a Summi Pontificis Legato in hac regione promulgationem, vim obligandi habitura esse."—*Acta et Decreta Primi Concilii Plenarii Indiae, Anno MCML in Bangalorensi Civitate Habiti* (Ranchi: Catholic Press, 1951), p. 22.

[25] Cocchi, *Commentarium*, III, 135.

[26] V. g., the promulgation made by the Apostolic Legate (1868) after the II Plenary Council of Baltimore (1886)—*Coll. Lac.*, III, 323-326; the promulgation made by the Apostolic Delegate on Dec. 12, 1928, after the approval of the decrees on June 12, 1928, of the I Plenary Council of China —*Primum Concilium Sinense, Anno 1924 a die 14 maii ad diem 12 junii in Ecclesia Scti. Ignatii de ZI-KA-WEI Celebratum* (Zi-ka-wei: Typographia Missionis Catholicae (T'ou-se-we), 1929), p. 20.

[27] S. C. S. Off., 10 sept. 1896, ad 2: "Utrum decreta Conciliorum sive

the press, or by means of any other agency, or their divulgement through preaching, are the various ways which a plenary council can use in spreading the knowledge of the law to its subjects.[28]

Canon 291, § 1, states, first of all, a positive command. It enjoins the presiding officer to transmit all the acts and decrees to the Holy See. Afterwards it states a prohibition. It forbids the promulgation of the decrees before the Sacred Congregation of the Council has examined or reviewed them. Does this mean that any attempt to promulgate the conciliar decrees without the required recognition would be not only unlawful but also invalid? If one consider the canon as it stands, simply incorporating a command together with the prohibition, it does not appear to contain an express or equivalent declaration of invalidity.[29] An equivalent expression of invalidity is found only where the very words of a law have some reference to invalidity, v. g., in a phrase such as "diriment impediment."[30] Supporting this opinion are distinguished canonists,[31] who explain the term *aequivalenter* of canon 11 as requiring that the text itself of the law must contain some verbal expression of nullity.[32]

There are also, however, authors who say that without the Holy

---

plenariorum sive provincialium a S. Sede *in forma communi sive specifica* confirmata, vel approbata, vel saltem recognita, omnimoda vi careant, nisi in statuta dioecesana iam fuerint incorporata, et quidem tantum valeant, in quantum sic fuerint incorporata. Ad 2. Negative.—Ssmus adprobavit."—*Fontes,* n. 1184. Cf. *Acta et Decreta Concilii Plenarii Quebecensis Primi* (*1909*), p. 482.

[28] Michiels, *Normae Generales,* I, 189.

[29] Canon 11.—Irritantes aut inhabilitantes eae tantum leges habendae sunt, quibus aut actum esse nullum aut inhabilem esse personam expresse vel aequivalenter statuitur.

[30] Vermeersch-Creusen, *Epitome,* I, 101.

[31] Van Hove, *De Legibus,* 168; Michiels, *Normae Generales,* I, 336 ff.; Toso, *Commentaria Minora,* I, 36; Beste, *Introductio,* p. 69; Roelker, "The Interpretation of Invalidating Laws," *The Jurist,* III (1943), 364-403, 377-402.

[32] V. g., can. 116: ". . . effectum non sortitur . . ."; can. 171, § 3: ". . . nihil est actum . . ."; for more, cf. Roelker, *Invalidating Laws* (Paterson: St. Anthony Guild Press, 1955), pp. 137-144.

See's antecedent recognition the promulgation of the conciliar decrees would be not only illicit but also invalid.[33]

The above mentioned canon is readily seen to form part of the constitutive common law which affects the plenary council. Its subject matter is identical with that of the former law. Hence it should be interpreted accordingly in the light of the former law.[34] Since pre-Code authors regarded the recognition of the conciliar decrees as a *conditio sine qua non* for the effective promulgation of the decrees, and as an indispensable element of the conciliar laws,[35] the writer believes that any promulgation without the required recognition prescribed by the cited canon would be invalid. Besides, the nature of the power of the council exceeds the episcopal power as such, and is dependent for its exercise upon the fulfillment of the conditions prescribed by the Holy Fathers; hence there arises the necessity of the fulfillment of the recognition of the conciliar decrees on the part of the Holy See.[36] The decrees thus legitimately promulgated become binding throughout the whole territory for which they were enacted on all persons whom they concern.

Article 3. Dispensation from the Conciliar Decrees

Canon 291.—§ 2. Decreta Concilii plenarii . . . promulgata obligent in suo cuiusque territorio universo, nec Ordinarii locorum ab iisdem dispensare possunt, nisi in casibus particularibus et iusta de causa.

---

[33] Wernz-Vidal, *Ius Canonicum,* II, 683; Coronata, *Institutiones,* I, 432; Chelodi, *Ius de Personis,* p. 373; Coronata, *Compendium,* I, p. 371, note 2.

[34] Canon 6, 2°.

[35] Wernz: *Ius Decretalium,* I, p. 279, note 42: "Ante recognitionem illam factam acta et decreta Concilii particularis promulgari valide non possunt." Petra, *Commentaria,* I, p. 284: "Et omnes docent, ut transmittantur statuta haec conciliaria Papae, qui solet ea approbare, medio oraculo, Sac. Congreg. Concilii, nec possunt imprimi, aut executioni demandari sine dicta facultate . . . ac est depositum in Constitutione Sixti V." Cf. Fagnanus, *Commentaria,* Lib. V, tit. 1, cap. 25, n. 95; Gousset, *Exposition des Principes du Droit Canonique* (Paris, 1859), p. 296; Scherer, *Handbuch des Kirchenrechtes* (2 vols., Graz-Leipzig, 1886-1898), I, 674.

[36] Toso, *Commentaria Minora,* III ,103, 110.

A dispensation is a relaxation of the law in a special case.[37] It removes the obligation of a law for certain persons, either physical or moral, things or circumstances, while the law itself remains intact and does not suffer abrogation or derogation, not only in so far as other subjects of the community are concerned, but even regarding the person dispensed, in those cases and circumstances for which he is not dispensed. The phrase *"in casu speciali,"* mentioned in canon 80, is similar to the phrase *in casibus particularibus* of canon 291, § 2.[38]

To grant a dispensation is an act of jurisdiction.[39] The power of dispensing belongs to the legislator, to his successor in office, or to the superior of the legislator, though these three persons can authorize a delegate who can utilize the same power.[40] They who receive delegated dispensatory power can use the said authority validly within the limits of their mandate.[41]

As has been said in the beginning of the previous chapter,[42] the laws of the plenary council bind throughout the whole territory for which the council is held, and emanate from a jurisdiction higher than that of an individual bishop. Individually taken the bishops are not the legislators of the plenary council, but rather the council as a whole, as constituted by them, forms a single legislative body. Thus, individual bishops of themselves do not have any power to dispense from any legislation enacted by the council.[43] Who, then, can give a dispensation from any of the laws of a plenary council? Canon 291, § 2, does not restrict the power of the local ordinary. Instead, it bespeaks for him a positive concession of dispensatory power as deriving from the law of the Code.[44] Therefore, on the assumption of two conditions, namely,

---

[37] Canon 80.

[38] Michiels, *Norma Generales, II,* 454.

[39] Maroto, *Institutiones,* I, 361.

[40] Canon 80.

[41] Cf. canon 203, § 1.

[42] Art. 1, p. 50.

[43] Suarez, *De Legibus,* Lib. VI, cap. 15, n. 4; Benedictus XIV, *De Synodo,* Lib. XIII, cap. 5, n. 8.

[44] Reilly, *The General Norms of Dispensation,* The Catholic University of America Canon Law Studies, n. 119 (Washington, D. C: The Catholic

a) in particular cases only, and b) for a just cause, bishops and other local ordinaries, by the law of the Code, can dispense from the laws of the plenary council. When either one of these two conditions is lacking, however, dispensations are both illicit and invalid, for then all operative dispensatory power is lacking.[45] The diocesan vicars general are included among the local ordinaries who can give dispensations from the conciliar decrees.[46] As this dispensatory power is attached to the office, it can be delegated accordingly to others by the local ordinaries.[47]

For the validity of every dispensation granted by an inferior from the law of his superior a just cause is needed.[48] Each time a legislator dispenses from his law without a cause he acts illicitly indeed, but nevertheless validly, because the whole obligation of the law depends on his will.[49] In the same way, he can give a general dispensation and even for an indefinite period of time, for he has the power to abrogate his own law. A dispensation from an enactment of a plenary council, however, is governed by the general principle stated in canon 84, § 3, that is, the dispensations granted without a just cause are both illicit and invalid. The restriction of the power of dispensing rests on the fact that the authority of a plenary council exceeds that of local ordinaries as such.[50]

As the granting of a dispensation is an act of voluntary non-judicial jurisdiction,[51] the local ordinary can dispense only those who are in some way his subjects[52] such as the *vagi* and *peregrini*[53]

University of America Press, 1939), p. 89 (hereafter cited as *General Norms*).

[45] Cf. canon 84, 1; Toso, *Commentaria Minora*, III, 111.

[46] Cf. canons 198; 368, § 1. It is to be recalled in this connection that the power of the vicar general of a residential bishop, of an Abbot *nullius*, or of a prelate *nullius* is not proper but vicarious.

[47] Cf. canons 199, § 1; Beste, *Introductio*, p. 255.

[48] Canon 84, § 1. Cf. Ojetti, *Commentarium in Codicem Iuris Canonici* (4 vols., Romae: Apud Aedes Universitatis Gregorianae, 1927-1931), I, 334.

[49] Maroto, *Institutiones*, I, 365.

[50] Coronata, *Institutiones*, I, n. 367.

[51] Cf. canon 201, § 3.

[52] Canon 82. Cf. also Wernz-Vidal, *Ius Canonicum*, I, 472.

[53] Cf. canons 14 and 91.

who are in his territory, and his own personal subjects by reason of domicile or quasi-domicile[54] though they be outside his territory. Local ordinaries may dispense even a whole diocese from the decrees of a plenary council, provided the dispensation is limited as to time. Moreover, local ordinaries can dispense individuals perpetually.[55]

It is most difficult to determine what constitutes a just cause for a dispensation, for the circumstances of places and persons must be considered according to the different gravity of each law. The grantor of a dispensation must weigh and consider carefully whether the alleged cause is reasonable and equitable with a view to a removal of the obligation of the law in each individual case.[56] It is not necessary that the cause be so weighty that it would of itself excuse from the observance of the law. In this case a dispensation is unnecessary.[57] What is required is that there be some reason which, while of itself it does not exempt from the law, is still sufficient to warrant in the prudent judgment of the superior the use of his power to make an exception in favor of one or more persons without, however, showing any favoritism.[58] In other words, whenever the observance of the lay would a) constitute a proportionately grave difficulty beyond the inconvenience one commonly experiences in abiding by a law, or b) impede some reasonably proportionate benefit which would result from the relaxation of the law, it can be said that a just cause exists.[59] The dispensation, nevertheless, could be granted, both licitly and validly, though the sufficiency of the cause given for dispensation is doubtful.[60]

---

[54] Cf. canon 94, § 1.

[55] Coronata, *Institutiones,* I, n. 369.

[56] Maroto, *Institutiones,* I, 365: "Sufficit ea causa, quae omnibus circumstantiis legis et personae consideratis, dignoscitur rationi conveniens, ita ut ex dispensatione concessa bonum commune non laedatur et bonum personae dispensatae augeatur." Cf. Guiniven, *The Precept of Hearing Mass,* The Catholic University of America Canon Law Studies, n. 158 (Washington, D. C.: The Catholic University of America Press, 1942), pp. 161-162.

[57] Reilly, *General Norms,* p. 107; Vermeersch-Creusen, *Epitome,* I, 170.

[58] Maroto, *Institutiones,* I, 365.

[59] Reilly, *op cit.,* p. 108.

[60] Canon 84, § 2; Reilly, *op. cit.,* p. 113.

Michiels furnishes an enumeration of different kinds of causes for the granting of a dispensation, as required in different parts of the Code.[61] Included among the causes which are sufficient for dispensations is the special class known as canonical causes, i.e., causes the sufficiency of which is recognized by the practice of the Roman Curia. A complete enumeration of the many causes which belong to this category cannot be made, although partial lists have been published at times. It must be remembered, however, that these enumerations of canonical causes are by no means intended to be complete lists. They are only demonstrative, since the Holy See explicitly calls them the principal canonical causes, meaning to say that there are other causes, not included in the lists, which are truly canonical and therefore sufficient to warrant dispensation.

Article 4. Interpretation of the Conciliar Decrees

The general rules given in the Code[62] must be observed in reference to the interpretation of the decrees of plenary councils. These rules give the right of interpretation to the legislators and their successors, and to those to whom they have committed the power to interpret the laws.[63] Thus, a plenary council can authentically interpret the decrees of a previous plenary council, for it has the power to make such laws, and is the legitimate successor of the preceding councils.

Authentic interpretation, which alone is considered here, is that which proceeds officially from a person in authority, so that it binds the subject to whom it is directed. If the interpretation is given in the form of a legal enactment it binds the whole community, but if the interpretation is given in the form of a judicial sentence or of a particular rescript it binds individual persons.[64]

Concerning individual bishops, it seems clear that apart from any delegation at all they cannot authentically interpret the decrees of plenary councils, since individually their legislative power does

[61] *Normae Generales,* II, 506, 567.

[62] Canon 17-20.

[63] Canon 17, § 1.—Leges authentice interpretatur legislator eiusve successor et is cui potestas interpretandi fuerit ab eisdem commissa.

[64] Cf. Van Hove, *De Legibus,* 251; canon 17, §§ 2, 3.

not extend to the enactments of the said council.[65] Moreover, an individual bishop does not intrinsically possess the power to issue an authentic interpretation *per modum legis.*[66] It seems also that a bishop could not authoritatively by way of rescript render an interpretation of the law of a plenary council considered in abstract, although the bishop can authentically interpret this legislation by judicial sentence.[67] Hence the *officialis*[68] can render a decision regarding plenary legislation. There does not seem to be in law a faculty whereby the bishop could interpret this legislation by means of the rescript of canon 17, § 3.

Maroto affirms that the plenary council can delegate the power of authentic interpretation to the members of the council collectively.[69] This view accords with canon 17, § 1, which says that the power of authentic interpretation can be delegated by the legislator.[70] Van Hove,[71] however, denies that the power of authentic intrepretation can be committed to the bishops as a group, apart from the exercise of such power of interpretation by the council itself in its actual sessions. He says that the legislative power of the plenary council is limited to the actual time of the celebration of the council. In reply it may be said that the laws of a plenary council continue to exercise their force after the close of the council, and it is only the enactment of new laws that would require the celebration of a new council. Therefore if the council delegated its power to interpret laws, this delegation would seem to continue in force even after the close of the plenary council.[72]

---

[65] Cf. canon 335, § 1.

[66] Schmidt, *The Principles of Authentic Interpretation in Canon 17 of the Code of Canon Law,* The Catholic University of America Canon Law Studies, n. 141 (Washington, D. C.: The Catholic University of America Press, 1941), p. 50 (hereafter cited as *The Principles of Authentic Interpretation*).

[67] Cf. canon 1570, § 1; Van Hove, *De Legibus,* 253, note 4: ". . . quia resoluto iure delegantis, nisi in duobus casibus de quibus in can. 61.

[68] Cf. canon 1573, § 2.

[69] *Institutiones,* I, 151.

[70] Cf. Toso, *Commentaria Minora,* I, 154.

[71] *De Legibus,* 253.

[72] Cf. canon 207, § 1.—Potestas delegata extinguitur . . . non autem resoluto iure delegantis, nisi in duobus casibus de quibus in can. 61.

Furthermore, it seems that the bishops as a group can be delegated by the council to give interpretations of the plenary decrees whenever the interpretations are of a merely declarative character, because a declarative interpretation is at most merely a paraphrase of the existing law; it states what is already, objectively, present in the law. The interpretation does not upon its appearance decree anything, rather it points out what has been decreed.

Accordingly, a declarative interpretation simply discovers what is already present in the anterior law and is therefore retroactive. The interpreting agent does not constitute a new rule of action; the source of obligation derives rather from the existing law than from the interpretation. Thus it supposes the law as already existing, and states what is already in the law from its inception.

Briefly, a declarative interpretation of law explains what is already present and it needs no promulgation.[73]

Authors have not considered the question whether bishops could be delegated to give in their own dioceses individual and independent authentic interpretations on the plenary laws. Such a measure would not seem feasible, since there should be not more than one source of authentic interpretation of plenary law within the territory for which the plenary council is being held.

In case a true *dubium iuris* concerning a conciliar decree should arise, the settlement by way of an authentic interpretation of this doubt may be referred to the Holy See, as the supreme legislator, or to a latter plenary council.[74]

---

[73] Cf. Schmidt, *The Principles of Interpretation*, p. 174.

[74] Cf. canon 17, § 1. Regarding this matter, the Fathers of the Latin-American Plenary Council laid down this rule, viz., that the bishops had power to settle doubts arising from the wording of the text so long as their interpretation did not affect the substance and juridical value of the same. In the latter case, the doubts were to be submitted to the Sacred Congregation for Extraordinary Affairs.—*Acta et Decreta Concilii Plenarii Americae Latinae (1899)*, n. 995.

CONCLUSIONS

1. The history of the Church testifies that the celebration of plenary councils became a constant practice and that the enforcement of its laws became acknowledged as an efficient means of administration. From within the councils came the norms and disciplinary measures for the faithtful outside. The councils taught, the faithful learned. Plenary councils may well be termed the guardians of the common law of the Church, for they played a specific part in the maintenance of the uniform observances of the common law.

2. From the fourth century of the Christian era until the present Code, the constant legislation of the Church concerning the celebration of plenary councils reflected their importance.

3. The Holy Father, himself, approves the time and the place selected for the celebration of a plenary council, or designates some other acceptable arrangement.

4. Only those members who under the law must be invited to the plenary council have the strict obligation to attend it.

5. The Code does not reserve any particular points to the plenary council.

6. A majority of the votes determines the conciliar decisions.

7. When the examination of the conciliar decrees has been executed by the Holy See no change is effected in the intrinsic nature of the decrees, nor does any correction of these decrees fortify them with any pontifical authority. The Holy See's recognition of the decrees serves simply as a safeguard in the framing of a uniform conciliar law.

8. For the licit and also the valid promulgation of the decrees, there is need of their recognition by the Holy See. The decrees can begin to bind either immediately upon their promulgation or after a short interval of time, in accord with whatever specific indication is given by the Fathers of the council.

9. Unless some contrary provision is expressly invoked, the

decrees of a plenary council revoke all contrary decrees of diocesan synods or provincial councils.

10. Individual bishops cannot authentically interpret the decrees of plenary councils. Any true *dubium iuris* regarding the conciliar decrees can be resolved by means of an authentic interpretation of the plenary council itself or of any higher authority.

BIBLIOGRAPHY

Sources

Acta Apostolicae Sedis, Commentarium Officiale, Romae, 1909—.

Acta et Decreta Concilii Plenarii Americae Latinae (1899), Romae: Typis Vaticanis, 1902.

Acta et Decreta Concilii Plenarii Baltimorensis Secundi (1866), 2. ed., Baltimorae, 1876.

Acta et Decreta Concilii Plenarii Baltimorensis Tertii (1884), 2. ed., Baltimorae, 1894.

Acta et Decreta Primi Concilii Plenarii Indiae (1950), Ranchi, 1951.

Acta et Decreta Concilii Plenarii Quebecensis Primi (1909), Quebeci, 1912.

Acta et Decreta Sacrorum Conciliorum Recentiorum, Collectio Lacensis, 7 vols., auctoribus G. Schneeman (Vol. I-VI), et T. Granderath (Vol. VII), Friburgi Brisgoviae, 1870-1890.

Acta Sanctae Sedis, 41 vols., Romae, 1865-1908.

Bouscaren, T. Lincoln, *The Canon Law Digest*, 3 vols. and supplement through 1954, Milwaukee, Wis.: The Bruce Publishing Company, 1934-1943, 1954, 1955.

Bruns, H. T., *Canones Apostolorum et Conciliorum Saeculorum IV-VII*, 2 vols., Berolini, 1839.

Bullarum Diplomatum et Privilegiorum Sanctorum Romanorum Pontificum Taurinensis Editio, 24 vols. in 25, 1857-1883, Vol. XIII, Neapoli, 1866.

Codex Iuris Canonici, Pii X Pontificis Maximi iussu digestus, Benedicti XV auctoritate promulgatus, Praefatione, Fontium Annotatione et Indice Analytico-Alphabetico ab Emo Petro Card. Gasparri Auctus, Romae: Typis Polyglottis Vaticanis, 1917; Reimpressio, 1946.

Codicis Iuris Canonici Fontes, cura Emi Petri Card. Gasparri editi, 9 vols., Romae: Typis Polyglottis Vaticanis, 1923-1939 (Vols. VII-IX, ed. cura et studio Emi Iustiniani Card. Serédi).

Collectanea S. Congregationis de Propaganda Fide, 2 vols., Romae: Typographia Polyglotta de Propaganda Fide, 1907.

Concilium Tridentinum, Diariorum, Actorum, Epistolarum, Tractatuum, Nova Collectio. Edidit Societas Goerresiana. 13 vols., Friburgi Brisgoviae: B. Herder, 1901-1950.

Constituciones del Segundo Sínodo de Lipa, Manila: Tip. Pont. de la Universidad de Sto. Tomás, 1948.

Constitution of the Republic of the Philippines, Manila, 1947.

Cursus Scriptorum Ecclesiasticorum Latinorum, incomplete, Vindibonae, 1866.

Decreta Authentica Congregationis Sacrorum Rituum, 5 vols., Romae: Ex Typographia Polyglotta, 1898-1901. Appendix II, 1927.

Decretales D. Gregorii Papae IX, suae integritati una cum glossis, Gregorii XIII Pont. Max. iussu editum, 2 vols., Romae, 1582.

Decretum Gratiani emendatum et notationibus illustratum cum glossis, Gregorii XIII Pont. Max. iussu editum, 2 vols., Romae, 1582.

Denzinger, H. et Umberg, J. B., *Enchiridion Symbolorum, Definitionum et Declarationum de Rebus Fidei et Morum*, 26. ed., Friburgi Brisgoviae: Herder & Co., 1947.

Fourth Diocesan Synod, Lafayette, La., 1953.

Griechischen christlichen Schriftsteller der ersten drei Jahrhunderte, Die, 7 vols. in 10, *Eusebius*, Vol. II, pars I (1903), pars II (1908), Leipzig.

Hardouin, Jean, *Acta Conciliorum et Epistolae Decretales ac Constitutiones Summorum Pontificum*, 12 vols., Parisiis, 1714-1715.

Mansi, Joannes, *Sacrorum Conciliorum Nova et Amplissima Collectio*, 53 vols. in 60, Paris, Arnhem, Leipzig, 1901-1927.

Monumenta Germaniae Historica, Gregorii I Papae Registrum Epistolarum, 2 vols. in 4, Berolini: Apud Weidmanos, 1891-1895.

Ordo in Concilio Plenario Servandus, Typis Polyglottis Vaticanis, 1946.

Pii X Pontificis Maximi Acta, 5 vols., Romae: Ex typographia Vaticana, 1905-1914; Vol. I, Romae, 1905.

Pontificale Romanum Summorum Pontificum iussu editum a Benedicto XIV et Leone XIII Pontificibus Maximis recognitum et castigatum, Mechliniae: H. Dessain, 1895.

Praxis Missionalis in Vicariatu Apostolico de Inchang, Wuchang: The Franciscan Press, 1935.

Primum Concilium Sinensis, A. D. MCMXXIV, Zi-Ka-Wei: Typographia Missionis Catholicae (T'ou-se-we), 1929.

Rituale Romanum, editio typica, Civitate Vaticana: Typis Polyglottis Vaticanis, 1952.

Sartori, Cosmas, *Enchiridion Canonicum*, 3. ed., emendata et aucta (1917-1932), Hankow: Missio Catholica, 1932.

Schroeder, H. J., *Canons and Decrees of the Council of Trent, Original Text with English Translations*, 2. ed., St. Louis: Herder, 1950.

Statutes of the Archdiocese of Dubuque, A.D. MCMXLVII.

The Holy Bible, New Catholic Edition, Westminster, Md.: The Newman Bookshop, 1955.

The Translation of Pius XII's Encyclical Letter on Sacred Music, Musicae Sacrae Disciplina, Dec. 25, 1955, Washington 5, D. C.: N.C.W.C. News Service.

Reference Works

Abbo, J.-Hannan, J., *The Sacred Canons,* 2 vols., St. Louis: Herder, 1952.

Aertnys, J.-Damen, C., *Theologia Moralis Secundum Doctrinam S. Alphonsi de Ligorio,* 11 ed., 2 vols., Taurinorum Augustae: Marietti, 1928.

Augustine, Charles, *A Commentary on the New Code of Canon Law,* 8 vols., 2. ed., St. Louis & London, 1918-1924; Vol. II, 1918; Vol. VI, 1923.

Ayrinhac, H., *Administrative Legislation in the New Code of Canon Law,* New York: Longmans, Green and Company, 1930.

———, *Constitution of the Church in the New Code of Canon Law,* New York: Blase Benziger and Company, Inc., 1925.

Bargilliat, M., *Praelectiones Juris Canonici,* 28. ed., ab auctore recognita et recentioribus decretis accomodata, 2 vols., Parisiis, 1913.

Baronius, Caesar, *Annales Ecclesiastici,* ed. A. Theiner, 37 vols., Vols. I-XXVIII, Barri-Ducis, 1864-1875; Vols. XXIX-XXXVII, Parisiis, 1876-1883.

Barrett, John, *A Comparative Study of the Councils of Baltimore and the Code of Canon Law,* The Catholic University of America Canon Law Studies, n. 83, Washington, D. C.: The Catholic University of America, 1932.

Benedictus XIV (Prospero Lambertini), *De Synodo Dioecesana,* 4 vols., Mechliniae, 1842.

Berutti, Christophorus, *Institutiones Iuris Canonici,* 6 vols. (Vol. I, Pars II, et Vol. V adhuc sub praelo), Taurini-Romae: Marietti, 1936-1943.

Beste, Uldalricus, *Introductio In Codicem,* 3. ed., Collegeville, Minn.: St. John's Abbey Press, 1946.

Blat, Albertus, *Commentarium Textus Codicis Iuris Canonici,* 5 vols. in 6, Romae, 1919-1927, Vol. II, De Personis, 1919; Vol. III, Partes II-VI, 1923.

Boffa, Conrad H., *Canonical Provisions for Catholic Schools,* The Catholic University of America Canon Law Studies, n. 117, Washington, D. C.: The Catholic University of America Press, 1939.

Bouix, Marie Dominique, *De Concilio Provinciali,* 3. ed., Parisiis, 1884.

Bouscaren, T.-Ellis, A., *Canon Law, A Text and Commentary,* 2. ed., Milwaukee: Bruce, 1951.

Brown, Brendan, *The Canonical Juristic Personality with special Reference to Its Status in the United States of America,* The Catholic University of America Canon Law Studies, n. 39, Washington, D. C.: The Catholic University of America, 1927.

Cance, A.-Arquer, M., *El Código de Decrecho Canónico,* 2 vols., Barcelona, 1934.

Capello, Felix M., *Summa Iuris Publici Ecclesiastici,* 3. ed., Romae: Apud Aedes Universitatis Gregorianae, 1932.

Caranza, Bartholomaeus, *Summa Conciliorum,* Duaci, 1639.

Cassotti, Mario, *Maestro e Scolaro-Saggio di Filosofia dell'Educazione,* Milano: Società Ed. "Vita e Pensiero," 1930.

Cavagnis, Felix, *Institutiones Iuris Publici Ecclesiastici,* 4. ed., 3 vols., Romae: Desclée, Lefebvre, et Soc., 1906.

Ceillier, Remy, *Histoire Générale des Auteurs Sacres et Ecclesiastiques,* 14 vols. in 17, Paris, 1858-1869.

Chelodi, Joannes, *Ius de Personis iuxta Codicem Iuris Canonici,* 3. ed. curavit Pius Ciprotti, Vicenza: Società Anonima Tipografica, 1942.

Cocchi, Guidus, *Commentarium in Codicem Iuris Canonci,* 8 vols. in 5, Vols. III & VI, 3. ed. recognita, Taurinorum Augustae: Marietti, 1931 & 1933.

Coleman, John, *The Minister of Confirmation,* The Catholic University of America Canon Law Studies, n. 125, Washington, D. C.: The Catholic University of America Press, 1941.

Coquia, Jorge R., *Legal Status of the Church in the Philippines,* Washington, D. C.: The Catholic University of America Press, 1950.

Coronata, Matthaeus Conte a, *Institutiones Iuris Canonici ad Usum Utriusque Cleri et Scholarum,* 5 vols., Taurini: Marietti, 1948-1952; Vols. I & II, 4. ed., 1950; Vol. III, 3. ed., 1948; Vol. IV, 3. ed., 1948; Vol. V, 3. ed., 1952.

———, *Compendium Iuris Canonici ad Usum Scholarum,* 3 vols., Taurini: Marietti, 1949-1950; Vol. I, 4. ed., 1950; Vol. II, 4. ed., 1950; Vol. III, 1949.

Das Holländische Schulgesetz, Düsseldorf, 1921, *in Schulpolitik und Erziehung: Zeitfragen,* Heft 11.

De Luca, M., *Institutiones Iuris Publici Ecclesiastici,* 2 vols., Romae, 1904.

De Meester, A., *Juris Canonici et Juris Canonico-Civilis Compendium,* ed. nova, 3 vols. in 4, Brugis: Sumptibus et Typis Societatis Sancti Augustini, 1921-1928.

Demeuran, J. Louis, *L'Eglise-Constitution-Droit Public,* Paris, 1914.

Eichman, Eduard, *Lehrbuch des Kirchenrechtes auf Grund des Codex Juris Canonici,* 6. ed., 3 vols., neu bearbeitet von Klaus Mörsdorf, Paderborn: Schönigh, 1949-1950.

Fagnanus, Prosper, *Commentaria in Quinque Decretalium Libros,* 5 vols. in 4, Venetiis, 1709.

Findlay, Stephen A., *Canonical Norms Governing the Deposition and Degradation of Clerics,* The Catholic University of America Canon Law Studies, n. 130, Washington, D. C.: The Catholic University of America Press, 1941.

Gabel, R. J., *Public Funds for Church and Private Schools,* Toledo, 1937.

Godts, F. X., *Les Droits en Matière d'Education,* 5 vols., Bruxelles, 1900-1901.

Gousset, Thomas, *Exposition des Principes du Droit Canonique,* Paris, 1859.

Granderath, T.-Kirch, C., *Geschichte des Vatikanischen Konzils von seiner ersten Ankündigung bis zu seiner Vertagung*, 3 vols., Friburg im Breisgau, 1903-1906.

Gredt, Joseph, *Elementa Philosophiae Aristotelico-Thomisticae*, 7. ed., 2 vols., Friburgi Brisgoviae: Herder, 1937.

Guilday, Peter, *The Life and Times of John England*, 2 vols., New York: The America Press, 1927.

———, *The National Pastorals of the American Hierarchy*, Westminster, Maryland: The Newman Press, 1954.

Guiniven, John, *The Precept of Hearing Mass*, The Catholic University of America Canon Law Studies, n. 158, Washington, D. C.: The Catholic University of America Press, 1942.

Hefele, Charles Joseph, *A History of the Christian Councils*, tr. by Wm. R. Clark, 5 vols., Edinburg: T. & T. Clark, 1876-1896.

Hefele, C.-Leclercq, H., *Histoire des Conciles* . . . nouvelle traduction francaise . . ., 11 vols. in 21, Paris, 1907-1952.

Hilgers, Joseph, *Der Index der verbotenen Buecher*, Freiburg im Breisgau, 1904.

Hinschius, Paul, *Das Kirchenrecht der Katholiken und Protestanten in Deutschland*, 6 vols., Berlin, 1869-1897.

Hostiensis (Henricus de Segusio), *Commentaria in Quinque Decretalium Libros*, 5 vols. in 3, Venetiis, 1581.

Hurley, Timothy, *A Commentary on the Present Index Legislation*, Dublin, 1908.

Kremer, Michael, *Church Support in the United States*, The Catholic University of America Canon Law Studies, n. 61, Washington, D. C.: The Catholic University of America, 1930.

Lischka, Charles N., *Private Schools and State Laws*, Washington, D. C.: The National Catholic Welfare Conference, 1926.

Lynch, George, *Coadjutors and Auxiliaries of Bishops*, The Catholic University of America Canon Law Studies, n. 238, Washington, D. C.: The Catholic University of America Press, 1947.

Magnin, E., "*L'Eglise Wisigothique au VIIe Siècle*, Vol. I, Paris: A. Picard et Fils, 1912.

Maroto, Philippus, *Institutiones Iuris Canonici ad Normam Novi Codicis*, 2 vols., Matriti-Romae-Barcinone, 1918-1919.

Martin, C., *Omnium Concilii Vaticani Quae ad Doctrinam et Disciplinam pertinet Documentorum Collectio*, Paderbornae, 1873.

McDonough, Thomas, *Apostolic Administrators*, The Catholic University of America Canon Law Studies, n. 139, Washington, D. C.: The Catholic University of America Press, 1941.

Michel, A., *La Question Scolaire et les Principes Théologiques*, Paris, Desclée, De Brouwer, 1921.

Michiels, Gomarus, *Normae Generales Juris Canonici,* 2 vols., ed. altera penitus retractata et notabiliter aucta, Tournai (Belg.): Desclée & Co., 1949.

———, *Principia Generalia de Personis in Ecclesia,* Lublin: Universitas Catholica, 1844-1864.

Monti, Giuseppe, *La Libertà della Scuola,* Milano: Soc. Ed. "Vita e Pensiero," 1928.

Moretti, Aloisius, *Coeremoniale iuxta Ritum Romanum seu de Sacris Functionibus Episcopo Celebrante, Assistente, Absente,* 4 vols., Taurini: Marietti, 1936-1939.

Murphy, Francis J., *Legislative Powers of the Provincial Council,* The Catholic University of America Canon Law Studies, n. 257, Washington, D. C.: The Catholic University of America Press, 1947.

Najera, Francisco Blanco, *Derecho Docente de la Iglesia, la familia, y el Estado,* Linares: Impr. "El Noticiero," 1934.

Nilles, Nicholas, *Commentaria in Concilium Plenarium Baltimorense Tertium, Praelectionibus Academicis Excerpta,* Oeniponte: F. Pustet, 1888.

Ojetti, Benedictus, *Commentarium in Codicem Iuris Canonici,* 4 vols., Romae: Apud Aedes Universitatis Gregorianae, 1927-1931.

———, *Synopsis Rerum Moralium et Iuris Pontificii,* 2 vols. in 1, 2. ed. emendata et aucta, Prati, 1904-1905.

Ottaviani, Alaphridus, *Institutiones Iuris Publici Ecclesiastici,* 2. ed., 2 vols., Typis Polyglottis Vaticanis, 1935-1936.

Petra, Vincentius, *Commentaria ad Constitutiones Apostolicas,* 5 vols. in 2, Venetiis, 1729.

Prümmer, Dominicus, *Manuale Iuris Canonici,* 4. & 5. ed., Friburgi Brisgoviae: Herder, 1927.

Reiffenstuel, Anacletus, *Jus Canonicum Universum,* 5 vols. in 7, Parisiis, 1864-1870.

Reilly, Edward, *The General Norms of Dispensation,* The Catholic University of America Canon Law Studies, n. 119, Washington, D. C.: The Catholic University of America Press, 1939.

Restrepo-Restrepo, Joannes M., *Concordata Regnante Sanctissimo Domino Pio PP. XI Inita,* Romae: Apud Aedes Pontificia Universitatis Gregorianae, 1934.

Roelker, Edward G., *Invalidating Laws,* Paterson, N. J.: St. Anthony Guild Press, 1955.

Romita, F., *Ius Musicae Sacrae,* Taurini: Marietti, 1936.

Santi, F.-Leitner, M., *Praelectiones Juris Canonici,* 5 vols. in 3, 4. ed., Ratisbonae, 1903-1905.

Scharnagl, A., *Religionsunterricht und Schule nach dem neuen kirchlichen Gesetzbuch,* 2. ed., M. Gladbach, 1923, in *Schulpolitik und Erziehung: Zeitfragen,* Heft 15.

Scherer, Rudolf Ritter von, *Handbuch des Kirchenrechtes,* 2 vols., Graz-Leipzig, 1886-1898.

Schmalzgrueber, Franciscus, *Ius Ecclesiasticum Universum,* 5 vols. in 12, Romae, 1843-1845.

Schmidt, John, *The Principles of Authentic Interpretation in Canon 17 of the Code of Canon Law,* The Catholic University of America Canon Law Studies, n. 141, Washington, D. C.: The Catholic University of America Press, 1941.

Sinco, V., *Philippine Government and Political Law,* Manila: Community Publishers, 1949.

Sipos, Stephanus, *Enchiridion Iuris Canonici,* 3. ed., Pécs: Ex Typographia "Haladas R. T.," 1936.

Smith, S., *Elements of Ecclesiastical Law,* 3 vols., Vol. III, New York, 1888.

Suarez, Franciscus, *Opera Omnia,* 28 vols., ed. L. Vivès, Parisiis, 1856-1861; Vols. V, VI, *De Legibus et Legislatore Deo.*

Terry, Charles Sanford, *Catholic Church Music,* London, 1907.

Thomassinus, Ludovicus, *Vetus et Nova Ecclesiae Disciplina circa Beneficia et Beneficiarios,* 3 partes in 10 vols., ed. postrema cum Parisiensi accuratissime collata, Magontiaci, 1787.

Toso, Albertus, *Ad Codicem Juris Canonici Commentaria Minora,* 5 vols. in 2, Vol. I, 2. ed. revisa, Torino-Roma, 1921, Vols. II-V, Romae: Jus Pontificium, 1922-1927.

Trombetta, Luigi, *De Consensu et Consilio Capituli Cathedralis iuxta Codicem Iuris Canonici,* Neapoli, 1926.

Van Hove, A., *Commentarium Lovaniense in Codicem Iuris Canonici,* 1 vol. in 5 tomes, Mechliniae: H. Dessain, Tom. II, *De Legibus Ecclesiasticis,* 1930.

Vermeersch, A.-Creusen, J., *Epitome Iuris Canonici,* 3 vols., Vol. I, 7. ed., Romae: H. Dessain, 1949.

Vito, P., *Note Canoniche sulla Precedenza,* Verona, 1924.

Wagner, J.-Andre, M., *Dictionnaire de Droit Canonique,* 5. ed., 4 vols., Paris: H. Walzer, 1901.

Wernz, F. X., *Ius Decretalium,* 6 vols., Vols. I-IV, Romae et Prati, 1908-1915; Vol. I, 3. ed., 1913; Vol. II, 3. ed., 1915; Vol. III, 2. ed., 1908; Vols. V-VI, 1. ed., Ojetti et Vidal, 1913-1914.

Wernz, F.-Vidal, P., *Ius Canonicum,* 7 vols. in 8, Romae: Apud Aedes Universitatis Gregorianae, 1934-1952; Vol. II, 3. ed., 1943; Vol. IV, Pars II, 1. ed., 1935; Vol. VII, 2. ed., 1951.

Wiest, Donald H., *Precensorship of Books,* The Catholic University of America Canon Law Studies, n. 329, Washington, D. C.: The Catholic University of America Press, 1953.

Winslow, Francis, *Vicars and Prefects Apostolic,* The Catholic Unuiversity of America Canon Law Studies, n. 24, Washington, D. C.: The Catholic University of America, 1924.

Woywod, S.-Smith, C., *A Practical Commentary in the Code of Canon Law,* revised ed., New York: Joseph F. Wagner, Inc., 1952.

Articles

Anonymus, "Annotationes," *Periodica,* XIV (1925), 180-182.

———, "From Foreign Reviews," *The Clergy Review,* XIV (1938), 89, 90.

Barrett, John, "Conciliar Laws Abrogated and Not Abrogated by the Code," *The Jurist,* II (1924), 62-67.

Creusen, J., "L'Ecole Catholique," *Nouvelle Revue Théologique,* LIII (1926), 184-200.

Goodwine, John A., "Problem Respecting the Censorship of Books," *The Jurist,* X (1950), 152-183; reprint edition (1950), pp. 1-34.

Hanrahan, P., "The Laws on Plenary Councils," *The Clergy Review,* XIV (1938), 387-402.

Letter of the Apostolic Delegate, Aug. 1, 1931—*Homiletic And Pastoral Review,* XXXII (1931), 189-190.

Roelker, Edward, "The Interpretation of Invalidating Laws," *The Jurist,* III (1943), 364-403.

Sacerdos, "The Pastor and His School Teachers," *Ecclesiastical Review,* LVII (1927), 12-30.

Schmid, L., "De Vi Verborum 'acatholicus, secta acatholica, minister acatholicus,' in Foro Canonico," *Apollinaris,* IV (1931), 552-567.

Periodicals

American Ecclesiastical Review, Vols. I-XXXII, Philadelphia, 1889-1905; from 1905: *The Ecclesiastical Review,* Vols. XXXIII-CIX, Philadelphia, 1905-1943; from 1944: *The American Ecclesiastical Review,* Washington, D. C., Vol. CX, 1944—

Apollinaris, Romae, 1928—

Clergy Review, The, London, 1931—

Homiletic and Pastoral Review, The, New York, 1900—(1900-1917: *Homiletic Monthly and Cathechist;* 1917-1918: *Homiletic Monthly;* 1918-1920: *Homiletic Monthly and Pastoral Review*).

Jurist, The, Washington, D. C., 1941—

Nouvelle Revue Théologique, Paris, 1869—

Periodica de Religiosis et Missionariis, 8 vols., Brugis, 1905-1919; *Periodica de Re Canonica et Morali utilia praesertim Religiosis et Missionariis,* 7 vols., Brugis, 1920-1927; *Periodica de Re Morali, Canonica, Liturgica,* Brugis, 1927-1936, et Romae, 1937—

The Register, Denver, Colorado, 1925—

ABBREVIATIONS

AAS—*Acta Apostolicae Sedis.*
ASS—*Acta Sanctae Sedis.*
Bruns—*Canones Apostolorum et Conciliorum Saeculormu* IV-VII.
Bull. Taur. Rom.—*Bullarum Diplomatum et Privilegiorum Romanorum Pontificum Taurinensis Editio.*
C.—Causa.
Can.—Canon.
cc.—Canons.
c. or cap.—caput.
C.I.C.—*Codex Iuris Canonici.*
Coll. Lac.—*Collectio Lacensis.*
Collectanea—*Collectanea Sacrae Congregationis de Propaganda Fide.*
CSEL—*Corpus Scriptorum Ecclesiasticorum Latinorum.*
D.—.Digesta Imperatoris Iustiniani or Distinctio.
Decr. Auth. S.R.C.—*Decreta Authentica Sacrae Congregationis Sacrorum Rituum.*
De Synodo—*De Synodo Dioecesana.*
Fontes—*Codicis Iuris Canonici Fontes.*
GCS—*Die Griechischen christlichen Schriftsteller der ersten drei Jahrhunderte.*
Law Digest—*Canon Law Digest and Supplement through* 1954.
Mansi—*Sacrorum Conciliorum Nova et Amplissima Collectio.*
MGH—*Monumenta Germaniae Historica.*
MPL—Migne, *Patrologiae Cursus Completus, Series Latina.*
n.—numero.
Periodica—*Periodica de Re Morali, Canonica, Liturgica.*
q.—quaestio.
S. C. de Prop. Fide—*Sacra Congregatio de Propaganda Fide.*
S. C. C.—*Sacra Congregatio Concilii.*
S. C. Consist.—*Sacra Congregatio Consistorialis.*
S. C. S. Off.—*Sacra Congregatio Sancti Officii.*
S. R. C.—*Sacrorum Rituum Congregatio.*

APPENDIX

PROFESSIO CATHOLICAE FIDEI

Ego N. firma fide credo et profiteor omnia et singula, quae continentur in symbolo Fidei, quo sancta Romana Ecclesia utitur, videlicet: Credo in unum Deum, Patrem omnipotentem, factorem caeli et terrae, visibilium omnium et invisibilium. Et in unum Dominum Iesum Christum, Filium Dei Unigenitum. Et ex Patre natum, ante omnia saecula. Deum de Deo, lumen de lumine, Deum verum de Deo vero. Genitum non factum, consubstantialem Patri: per quem omnia facta sunt. Qui propter nos homines, et propter nostram salutem descendit de caelis. Et incarnatus est de Spiritu Sancto ex Maria Virgine, et Homo factus est. Crucifixus etiam pro nobis, sub Pontio Pilato: passus et sepultus est. Et resurrexit tertia die, secundum Scripturas. Et ascendit in caelum: sedet ad dexteram Patris. Et iterum venturus est cum gloria iudicare vivos, et mortuos: cuius regni non erat finis. Et in Spiritum Sanctum, Dominum et vivificantem: qui ex Patre Filioque procedit. Qui cum Patre et Filio simul adoratur, et conglorificatur: qui locutus est per prophetas. Et Unam, Sanctam, Catholicam et Apostolicam Eccclesiam. Confiteor unum Baptisma in remissionem peccatorum. Et exspecto resurrectionem mortuorum. Et vitam venturi saeculi. Amen.

Apostolicas et ecclesiasticas traditiones, reliquasque eiusdem Ecclesiae observationes et constitutiones firmissime admitto et amplector. Item sacram Scripturam iuxta eum sensum, quem tenuit et tenet sancta Mater Ecclesia, cuius est iudicare de vero sensu et interpretatione sacrarum Scripturarum, admitto; nec eam unquam, nisi iuxta unanimem consensum Patrum, accipiam et interpretabor.

Profiteor quoque septem esse vere et propie Sacramenta novae legis a Iesu Christo Domino nostro instituta, atque ad salutem humani generis, licet non omnia singulis necessaria, scilicet, Baptismum, Confirmationem, Eucharistiam, Poenitentiam, Extremam

Unctionem, Ordinem et Matrimonium; illaque gratiam conferre, et ex his Baptismum, Confirmationem et Ordinem sine sacrilegio reiterari non posse. — Receptos quoque et approbatos Ecclesiae Catholicae ritus in supradictorium omnium Sacramentorum sollemni administratione recipio et admitto. — Omnia et singula quae de peccato originali et de iustificatione in sacrosancta Tridentina Synodo definita et declarata fuerunt, amplector et recipio. — Profiteor pariter in Missa offerri Deo verum, proprium et propitiatorium Sacrificium pro vivis et defunctis; atque in sanctissimo Eucharistiae Sacramento esse vere, realiter et substantialiter Corpus et Sanguinem una cum anima et divinitate Domini nostri Iesu Christi, fierique conversionem totius substantiae panis in Corpus, et totius substantiae vini in Sanguinem, quam conversionem Catholica Ecclesia Transubstantiationem appellat. Fateor etiam sub altera tantum specie totum atque integrum Christum, verumque Sacramentum sumi. — Constanter teneo Purgatorium esse, animasque ibi detentas fidelium suffragiis iuvari. Similiter et Sanctos una cum Christo regnantes venerandos atque invocandos esse, eosque orationes Deo pro nobis offerre, atque eorum Reliquias esse venerandas. Firmiter assero imagines Christi ac Deiparae semper Virginis, necnon aliorum Sanctorum habendas et retinendas esse, atque eis debitum honorem ac venerationem impertiendam. — Indulgentiarum etiam potestatem a Christo in Ecclesia relictam fuisse, illarumque usum Christiano populo maxime salutarem esse affirmo. — Sanctam, Catholicam et Apostolicam Romanam Ecclesiam, omnium Ecclesiarum matrem et magistram agnosco, Romanoque Pontifici beati Petri Apostolorum Principis successori ac Iesu Christi Vicario veram obedientiam spondeo ac iuro.

Cetera item omnia a sacris Canonibus et Oecumenicis Conciliis, ac praecipue a sacrosancta Tridentina Synodo et ab Oecumenico Concilio Vaticano tradita, definita ac declarata, praesertim de Romani Pontificis primatu et infallibili magisterio, indubitanter recipio atque profiteor, simulque contraria omnia, atque haereses quascunque ab Ecclesia damnatas et reiectas et anathematizatas, ego pariter damno, reiicio et anathematizo. Hanc veram Catholicam Fidem, extra quam nemo salvus esse potest, quam in praesenti sponte profiteor et veraciter teneo, eandem integram et inviolatam usque ad extremum vitae spiritum, constantissime, Deo adjuvante, retinere et confiteri, atque a meis subditis seu illis, quorum cura ad me in munere meo spectabit, teneri et doceri et praedicari, quantum in me erit curaturum, ego idem N. spondeo, voveo ac iuro. Sic me Deus adiuvet, et haec sancta Dei Evangelia.

ALPHABETICAL INDEX

Abbots *nullius*, 33, 35
Absence from councils, 37, 39, 42
  See also Procurators
Abuses, correction of, 16, 51, 58
Adjournment of council, 32
Administrators, apostolic, 33, 35 ff., 39
Appeals,
  from metropolitan to designated suffragan, 64
  from suffragan to the metropolitan, 64
  in devolutivo, 64
Archbishop,
  right of precedence, 44 ff.
  with deliberative vote, 33
Attendance at councils,
  excusing causes for, 37, 39, 41
  obligatory for voting members, 33 ff., 36
  when obligatory for others, 33 ff., 39

Baltimore,
  II Plenary Council, 79
  III Plenary Council, 79
Begging, by priests, 70, 71 fn. 101, 72
Bishops, 3 ff., 19, 23 ff.
  coadjutor or auxiliary, 33, 36 ff., 40 ff.
  election of, 10
  interpretation of conciliar decrees by, 104 ff.
  residential, 33, 36, 39, 54
  titular,
    cannot send procurators, 37 ff.
    obliged to attend plenary council, 41 ff.
    precedence of, 44
    without right to attend plenary council, 37 ff.
Books,
  censorship of, 89 ff.
  diocesan censors of, 91
  prohibition of, 92 ff.
    effect of, 92
    force of, 92
Business, among clerics, 66

Canonists, 38
Cardinal Legate, precedence, 43 ff.
Catholic schools,
  and its teachers, 87 ff.
  duty to attend only, 80 ff.
  establishment of, 78 ff.
  faithful and, 83 ff.
  parents and, 86 ff.
  pastors and, 85 ff.
  support of, 82 ff.
  the state and, 83, 88
Censorship of books,
  right of the Church on, 90 ff.
  right of the State on, 89
Chimes, 76
Church,
  power of, to teach, 56
  right of,
    to establish schools, 78 ff.
    to forbid books, 89 ff.
  supremacy of, in spiritual matters, 12, 56
Clergy,
  attending councils, 10, 37 ff.
  reputation of, 11, 64 fn. 73, 65 fn. 75, 66 fn. 76, 67 ff.
Collegiate moral person or *collegium*, 26 ff.
Conciliar decrees,
  deliberation of, 59 ff., 94
  determining, 54
  dispensation from, 18 ff., 101 ff.
  examining, 94 ff.
  interpreting, 104 ff.
  promulgation of, 17, 94, 97, 98 footnotes 23, 24, 26
  recognition of, 17, 94 ff., 100, 100 fn. 35
  strength of, 17 ff., 50, 94, 96 fn. 11, 97
  subject of, 34, 50 ff., 97
  suspension after promulgation, 95 fn. 4
  territoriality of, 51, 94, 100
Concursus,
  aim of the, 62
  conferring of parishes by, 61 ff.
  general, 61
  means of expediting the, 63 ff.
  norms for the, 63
  special, 61

Conferences of bishops, 60
Controversies,
dogmatic, 4, 16, 51 ff.
settlement of, 4, 51, 56 ff.
Councils,
celebration of, 7
convocation of, 5, 29
ecumenical, 3, 5, 16, 24 ff.
meaning of, 3
national, 3, 6 ff., 12 ff., 25
patriarchal, 3
presiding at, 3, 24
primatial, 3
provincial, 3, 5, 9, 24 ff., 29 ff., 60

Decisions of council, 50, 53 ff.
Degradation, 70 ff.
Departure, premature, from council, 42
Deposition, 70 ff.
Deprivation,
benefice or office, 71
perpetual, clerical garb, 71
right connected with office or benefice, 71
Diocesan synod, 60
Discipline, uniformity of, 51, 59 ff.
Dispensation,
causes required for, 101 ff., 104
defined, 101
persons who can give, 101 ff.
subject of, 102 ff.
Dubium iuris, 53, 106

Education,
Catholic church in, 78, 81 ff., 87
Catholic, in the Philippines, 78 ff., 83
Catholic, in the United States, 78 ff., 83
Role of Sisters in Catholic, 88
Eusebius, 4, 9
Examination, for parish, 61 ff.

Faith,
increase of, 51 ff., 56 ff.
profession of, at councils, 46 ff.
purity of, 85
Force of conciliar decrees,
superior to decrees of individual bishops and local ordinaries, 50
surpassing all episcopal and synodical laws, 50
Frequency of councils,
how observed, 28 ff.
in Italy, 28
laws prescribing, 5 ff.

Gregorian chant, 74, 76
Germany, 32, 90

Heresies,
checked by councils, 57
condemnation of, 4, 57
Holy Office,
on censorship of books, 91 ff.
Hostiensis, 7

Indult, requested by councils, 53, 67 ff.
Interpretation of conciliar decrees, 18, 104
delegated, 104 ff.
merely declarative, 106
removing a *dubium iuris,* 106
Italy, plenary councils instead of provincial in, 28

Jurisdictional powers of plenary councils, 50, 55

Kenrick, Francis P., 25

Laity and clerics, distinction, 10, 71 fn. 102
Latin America, plenary council of,
on Catholic schools, 85 ff.
on interpretation of conciliar decrees, 106
Laws,
contra legem superiorem, 52 ff.
disciplinary, 57 ff.
doubtful, 53
praeter ius commune, 52 fn. 17, 53
praeter legem superiorem, 52 ff.
Legate of the Holy See, 15, 28 ff., 32 ff., 36 ff., 42 ff., 46, 54, 55
Leo XIII, Pope,
on Catholic schools, 81 ff.
on censorship of books, 85 ff.
Limitations of conciliar decrees, 51 ff.
Liturgical music, 76
Local ordinary, the,
and Catholic schools, 84 ff.
and sacred music, 76
as members of the conciliar assembly, 34
distinguished from religious ordinary, 34
even *sede impedita,* 35
giving dispensations, 101 ff.

limitation of his jurisdiction, 34
on censure of books, 91 ff.
on his right to vote, 33 ff.
supporting a suspended priest, 73

Major cleric, reduction to lay state, 71
Majority vote required, 54
Manila, provincial council, 79
Members, conciliar, requisite number of, 31
Methods of legislation,
preliminary sessions, 60
preparatory commissions, 60
regular meetings of bishops, 60
Metropolitans,
convoking councils, 5, 29
presiding at councils, 3, 24
Mission territories, councils in, 96
Modernism, oath against, 48
Monastic congregations, superiors of, 35 ff.
Morality, books attacking, 89 ff.
Morals,
preservation of, 51 fl., 57 ff.
purity of, 85

Negotiatio, forbidden to clerics, 66 ff.
New York, Archbishop of, 76
Non-Catholics, in Catholic schools, 81, 87 ff.
Non-residents, when bound by laws, 102 ff.
Notaries, 38
Nuns, 88

Oath against modernism, 48
Obduracy in censures, 68, 70 ff.
Objects of conciliar legislation,
general, 54 ff.
particular, 69 ff.
Opening of council, 32, 53
Organ, electric, 76
Oriental rite, the,
bishops and priests of, 45
churches of, 92

Papal approbation of conciliar decrees, 17, 94 ff.
Patriarchs, 3, 9, 30 ff., 44, 47
Peals, 76
Penalties,
circumstances considered, 69
classification of, 68 ff.
infliction of, 68 ff.
observance of, 69
peculiar, to clerics, 71
power to inflict, 68
those which the local ordinary may enact, 71
Peregrini, 102
Place of council, 27 ff.
factors to be considered in, 28
no special provision, 28
Plenary council,
adjournment of, 32, 53
authority of, 14, 26 ff., 51 fn. 32, 52
business discussed in the, 6, 10, 14, 16, 53, 55 fn. 33, 57, 60
competence of, 51 ff.
concept of, 3, 5, 23 ff., 55
convocation and presidency of, 9, 14, 29 ff., 32 ff., 54
distinguished,
from ecumenical council, 3, 24 ff., 32
from provincial council, 3, 24
frequency of celebrating, 5 ff., 12, 29
history of, 3
jurisdiction of, 51
legislative power of, 50, 52, 55
not a *collegium,* 27
number of members required for, 31
opening of, 27 ff., 53
operation of, 9 ff.
origin of, 4
permission for celebrating, 31, 32 fn. 52
persons to be called to the, 9
place for, 27 ff.
powers of, 11, 50, 52
precedence in, 10, 15
procedure at, 53
quorum not required for, 54 ff.
time for, 27 ff., 53
transfer of, 32, 53
utility of, 6, 11, 29
vote required at, 54, 60
Polyphony, 76
Pontifical household, precedence, 43
Popes, on councils, 7 ff., 12, 23, 29
Precedence,
among archbishops, 44 ff.
among bishops, 44 ff.
among cardinals, 43 ff.
among prelates, 44 ff.
among priests, 44 ff.
among procurators, 45

controversy over, 45
in plenary councils, 10, 15, 43 ff.
meaning of, 43
necessity of, 42
norms of, 43
where to be observed, 45
Prefects apostolic, 33 fn. 61
Prelates *nullius,* 33
Presiding at plenary councils, 32, 53 ff.
Primates, 3, 9, 30 ff.
Privileges, of clerics,
division of, 71 fn. 102
how lost, 72 fn. 102
manner of acquiring, 71 fn. 102
renunciation of, 71 fn. 102
Procurators,
lacking deliberative vote, 39 ff.
mandate required by, 37,39
possessing deliberative vote, 37 ff.
precedence of, 45
selection of, 39
qualifications of, 37, 40
selection of, 39
without a double vote, 39
Profession of faith,
formula prescribed, 48 ff., 118 ff.
how it should be made, 46 ff.
obligation of the, 46 ff.
persons obliged to make the, 47 ff.
when prescribed, 46
Prohibition of books, 92 ff.
and its effects, 92
particular councils on, 92
Promulgation,
defined, 97
mode of, 17, 97 ff.
time of, 99
See also Recognition of Decrees
Pro-prefects apostolic, 34 ff.
Protracting of conciliar session, 32, 53
Pro-vicars apostolic, 34, 35
Province, ecclesiastical, 3 ff., 24 ff.
Public schools, 77 ff.

Quasi-domicile, 37 ff., 103

Recognition of decrees, 17, 94
kinds of, 94 ff.
how it is done, 95 ff.
purpose of, 95 ff.
See also Promulgation
Recourse against a conciliar decree, 93
Reduction to lay state, 71
Relevant legislation, 9 ff., 50, 57 ff.
Residence,
prescribed or forbidden, as penalty, 69
prescribed outside diocese, 70
how determined, 37 ff., 103
Retreat house, for clergy, 69

Sacred music,
and musical instruments, 75 ff.
church's interest in, 74
in divine worship, 74 ff.
liturgical laws on, 74, 76
pastors and, 75 ff.
plenary council and, 76
qualities of, 74 ff.
St. Pius X on, 74, 76 ff.
Schools,
and the church, 82
and the parents, 78
and the state, 78, 83
anti-Catholic, 80
Catholic, 78
curriculum in the, 81
lay, 80
mixed, 80 ff.
neutral, 80 ff.
non-Catholic, 80 ff.
private, 77, 85
public, 77, 80, 95
Superiors general, 35 ff.
Suspension, 70 ff.
from office, 71
its importance, 69
kinds of, 71
Synods,
diocesan, publishing conciliar decrees, 98
held every year, 5, 6
held in the second century, 4

Teaching, office of the church, 56 ff.
Territoriality of conciliar decrees, 51, 94, 100
Territory divisions, 25, 51
Tertullian, 3
Theologians, 38
Time for council, 27 ff.
Tonsure, 44
Transfer of council, 32, 53
Trent, Council of, 47 ff„ 55, 63

Uniformity of discipline, 23, 59 ff.
Utility of councils, 51 ff., 60 ff.

Vagi, 102
Vicars apostolic, 33 fn. 61
Vicars capitular, 33 fn. 62
  appointments of, 35
  right to a deliberative vote, 35
Vicars general,
  can give dispensations from conciliar decrees, 102
  not conciliar members; 34
Vote,
  consultative, 38 ff., 48 ff.
  deliberative, 33 fn. 59, 36 ff., 40 ff., 48 ff., 54
  how constituted, 26
Voting,
  apostolic legate's single vote, 55
  majority required, 54
  order of, 45.

BIOGRAPHICAL NOTE

ELIAS OLARTE POBLETE was born in Mabitac, Laguna, the Philippines, on December 1, 1921. He began the primary grades in his home town. After finishing his elementary school education in Siniloan, Laguna, he entered St. Francis of Sales Minor Seminary in San Pablo City on June 13, 1935, graduating therefrom in March, 1939. In June of the same year he entered the Diocesan Seminary of St. Alphonsus Maria de Ligorio in Lipa City, where he completed his philosophical and theological studies. On June 15, 1945, the Most Rev. Alfredo Verzosa († June 27, 1954) sent him to the School of Canon Law of the University of Santo Tomás, Manila, where he received the degree of Baccalaureate in Canon Law in March of the following year. He was ordained to the holy priesthood on March 16, 1946, for the diocese of Lipa. Immediately after his ordination he was assigned as pastor of his home town and at the same time as administrator of a neighboring parish in a nearby town. He was engaged in parish work until June, 1950. From July, 1950, until April, 1954, he served as Prefect of Discipline and Professor at the Diocesan Seminary, his own *alma mater*. In September, 1954, he entered the School of Canon Law at the Catholic University of America. He received the degree of the Licentiate in Canon Law in June, 1955.

CANON LAW STUDIES*

368. Bockstie, Rev. Richard, C.Ss.R., J.C.L., The principal oratory of religious.
369. Grajewski, Rev. Maurice J., O.F.M., M.A., Ph.D., J.C.L., The supreme moderator of exempt religious orders.
370. Havlik, Rev. Bernard J., A.B., J.C.L., The cessation of rescripts.
371. Olkovikas, Rev. Albert William, S.T.L., J.C.L., The *instantia* of the lawsuit.
372. Poblete, Rev. Elias Olarte, J.C.L., The plenary council.
373. Sokolovich, Rev. Alexander F., S.T.L., J.C.L., Canonical provisions for universities and colleges.
374. Sullivan, Rev. Jordan J., O.F.M.Cap., B.A., J.C.L., Fast and abstinence in the First Order of St. Francis.

* For a complete list of the available number of this series apply to The Catholic University of America Press, 620 Michigan Ave., N.E., Washington (17), D.C., for a general catalogue.

www.ingramcontent.com/pod-product-compliance
Lightning Source LLC
LaVergne TN
LVHW050209080826
844660LV00012B/384